MW00613905

Growth, Inequality, and Globalization
Theory, History, and Policy

The question of how inequality is generated and how it reproduces over time has been a major concern for social scientists for more than a century. Yet the relationship between inequality and the process of economic development is far from being well understood.

These Raffaele Mattioli Lectures have brought together two of the world's leading economists, Professors Philippe Aghion (a theorist) and Jeffrey Williamson (an economic historian), to question the conventional wisdom on inequality and growth, and address its inability to explain recent economic experience. Professor Aghion assesses the affects of inequality on growth, and asks whether inequality matters: if so why is excessive inequality bad for growth, and is it possible to reconcile aggregate findings with macroeconomic theories of incentives? In the second part Jeffrey Williamson discusses the Kuznets hypothesis, and focuses on the causes of the rise of wage and income inequality in developed economies.

PHILIPPE AGHION is Professor of Economics at University College London and Senior Economist at the European Bank for Reconstruction and Development. He is the managing editor of *Economics of Transition*, and has recently co-authored *Endogenous Growth Theory* with Peter Howitt (MIT Press, 1998).

JEFFREY G. WILLIAMSON is Laird Bell Professor of Economics at Harvard University. He is the author of numerous books and articles including, *The Age of Mass Migration: An Economic Analysis* with T.J. Hatton (Oxford University Press, 1997).

Growth, Inequality, and Globalization

Theory, History, and Policy

Philippe Aghion
University College London

and

Jeffrey G. Williamson
Harvard University

CAMBRIDGE
UNIVERSITY PRESS

PUBLISHED BY THE PRESS SYNDICATE OF THE UNIVERSITY OF CAMBRIDGE
The Pitt Building, Trumpington Street, Cambridge, United Kingdom

CAMBRIDGE UNIVERSITY PRESS
The Edinburgh Building, Cambridge CB2 2RU, UK
40 West 20th Street, New York, NY 10011–4211, USA
10 Stamford Road, Oakleigh, VIC 3166, Australia
Ruiz de Alarcón 13, 28014 Madrid, Spain
Dock House, The Waterfront, Cape Town 8001, South Africa

http://www.cambridge.org

© BANCA COMMERCIALE ITALIANA 1998

This book is in copyright. Subject to statutory exception
and to the provisions of relevant collective licensing agreements,
no reproduction of any part may take place without
the written permission of Cambridge University Press.

First published 1998
Reprinted 2000, 2001

Printed in the United Kingdom at the University Press, Cambridge

Typeset in 9.5/13pt Utopia

A catalogue record for this book is available from the British Library

Library of Congress Cataloguing in Publication data
Aghion, Philippe.
  Growth, inequality and globalization : theory, history, and policy / Philippe
Aghion and Jeffrey G. Williamson.
      p.   cm. – (Raffaele Mattioli lectures)
    Includes index.
    ISBN 0 521 65070 4 (hardbound)
    1. Economic development.   2. Income distribution.   I. Williamson,
Jeffrey G., 1935–   II. Title.   III. Series.
    HD75.A339   1998
    338.9–dc21   98-29551
                      CIP

ISBN 0 521 65070 4 hardback
ISBN 0 521 65910 8 paperback

Contents

Preface

The Raffaele Mattioli Lectures, in which many prominent economists have taken part, were established in 1976 by Banca Commerciale Italiana in association with Università Commerciale Luigi Bocconi as a memorial to the cultural legacy left by Raffaele Mattioli, for many years chairman of the bank.

The aim of the new series of Lectures, which is not only promoted by Banca Commerciale Italiana and Università Commerciale Luigi Bocconi but also supported by Università Cattolica del "Sacro Cuore" (Milan), Università degli Studi di Milano and Politecnico di Milano, is to create an opportunity for reflection and debate on topics of particular current interest, thus providing stimuli and ideas for the increasing challenges of a continually changing worldwide economic scenario.

The present initiative is therefore dedicated to the analysis of the effects of important changes which are now taking place in the world economy: the globalisation of markets, the continuous evolution in the field of information, technology and communications and the convergence of economics and international relations.

It is evident that these changes, coupled with the forthcoming European Monetary Union, provide many complex subjects that will be best dealt with from an interdisciplinary perspective.

Distinguished academics and researchers of all nationalities concerned with all kinds of economic problems will be invited to take part in this enterprise, with the intention of contributing to the debate interconnecting economic theory with practical policy.

These lectures were presented in abbreviated form on November 20, 1997 at the Banca Commerciale Italiana (Milan) and on November 21, 1997 at Bocconi University (Milan). We are grateful for the efficient and cheerful staff at BCI and Bocconi, and for the useful comments from the discussants during the second day: Franco Amatori, Carlo Dell'Aringa, Francesco Giavazzi, Gianni Toniolo and Ignazio Visco.

Philippe Aghion, London, UK
Jeffrey G. Williamson, Cambridge, USA

Introduction

One of us is a theorist, and one of us is an historian, but both of us are economists interested in modern debates about technical change, convergence, globalization, and inequality. The central bridge that spans theory and history over these debates is the Kuznets Curve.

In his Presidential address to the American Economic Association more than forty years ago, Simon Kuznets (1955) posed an hypothesis that still commands central attention in the pages of our journals. Kuznets suggested that in the long run, modern economic growth would generate an early industrialization phase of rising inequality, followed eventually by a mature industrialization phase of declining inequality. His idea was that income and wealth inequality within any country should tend to trace out an inverted U, a prediction subsequently called the Kuznets Curve.

Four decades ago, Kuznets had very little evidence to perform anything but a crude test of his hypothesis, and thus he was cautious. Yet, he was able to document falling inequality in many OECD countries in this century, some with the fall starting around World War I, some postponing the fall until 1929, but all sharing a revolutionary leveling of income and wealth from the 1920s to the 1960s. True, his evidence documenting a nineteenth century upswing of the Kuznets Curve was fragmentary at best, and he

1

was not able to offer any evidence for either side of the Kuznets Curve for countries in East Europe, the Middle East, Latin America, Asia or Africa. In any case, debate about the facts has been intense ever since, perhaps because capitalism seems to be on trial.

World Bank economists writing in the 1970s thought limited postwar data confirmed the Kuznets Curve, but better data and empirical methods subsequently dashed that confidence. Economic historians writing in the 1970s and 1980s thought limited data for Britain since 1760 and the United States since 1776 also confirmed the Kuznets Curve, but more and better evidence collected since has tended to erode that bold view, especially the evidence of a sharp rise in wage inequality in most OECD countries since the early 1970s.

Before an obituary for the Kuznets Curve is written, however, we should note how narrow has been the focus of this traditional literature. Kuznets derived his hypothesis by appealing to the factor demand effects generated by an economy's transition from traditional agriculture to modern industry. He offered reasons why this process should be labor saving, and unskilled labor saving in particular: when the transition is fast, labor saving should be dramatic and inequality should rise; when the transition is slow or complete, labor saving should evaporate and inequality should fall. Kuznets used "development" and GDP per capita levels as proxies for these (unskilled) labor-saving effects. Even if the proxies have turned out to be imperfect, and even if there have been important offsetting forces at work, absence of an inverted U does not necessarily imply absence of these labor-saving, demand-side forces. Kuznets' (unskilled) labor-saving effects may still be at work even in the absence of the Kuznets Curve.

What we need is less effort at establishing or rejecting the Kuznets Curve as a stylized fact, and more effort at uncovering the sources of inequality change. And there is absolutely no reason why the sources of inequality change cannot be identified the same way that macroeconomists have recently identified the sources of growth. What are the underlying forces that might cause rising inequality? The big three commonly put forward to explain the recent inequality surge are trade, technology, and labor supply. Which factor has been most important in the recent past? Can the same three forces also explain inequality trends over the past two hundred years?

Part I (Aghion) and Part II (Williamson) of this book confront all of these issues. The first relies more on theory while the second relies more on history, but both are motivated by the same questions. What accounts for growth and inequality? How are they related? How does globalization influence both? While policies and institutions may have a clear impact on growth and inequality, to what extent do growth and inequality have an impact on policies and institutions? The chapters in this book offer some answers. While the answers are tentative and qualified, we hope they will at least serve to stimulate further work on what are surely fundamental questions about the human condition.

PART ONE
Inequality and economic growth

Philippe Aghion
with Cecilia García-Peñalosa
and Eve Caroli

1 Introduction

The question of how inequality is generated and how it reproduces over time has been a major concern for social scientists for more than a century. Yet the relationship between inequality and the process of economic development is far from being well understood. In particular, for the past forty years conventional economic wisdom on inequality and growth has been dominated by two fallacies:

(a) On the effect of inequality on growth in market economies, the standard argument is that inequality is *necessarily* good for incentives and therefore good for growth, although incentive and growth considerations might (sometimes) be traded off against equity or insurance aims.

This conventional wisdom has been challenged by a number of recent empirical studies. Several papers have used cross-country regressions of GDP growth on income inequality to examine the correlation between these two variables. Alesina and Rodrik (1994), Persson and Tabellini (1994), Perotti (1996), and Hausmann and Gavin (1996b) have all found that there is a negative correlation between average growth and measures of inequality over the 1960–1985 period (although the relationship is stronger for developed than for developing countries). Persson and Tabellini (1994) also present time-series evidence for nine developed economies over the period 1830–1985: their results show that inequality has a negative impact on growth at *all* the stages of development that these economies have gone through in the past 150 years (see Benabou (1996) for a comprehensive review of the literature).

This part draws heavily from joint work with Patrick Bolton, Peter Howitt, and GianLuca Violante. We also benefitted from numerous discussions with Beatriz Armendariz, Tony Atkinson and Roland Benabou, and from the comments of Juan Antonio García, Jon Temple, and Andrea Richter. Finally, we wish to thank the "Cost of Inequality" group of the McArthur Foundation and the School of Public Policy at UCL for invaluable intellectual and financial support.

Table 1. *Korea and the Philippines*

	Gini (%)	Q1	Q2	Q3	Q4	Q5	Q3–Q4	Q5/Q1	Q5/Q1–Q2
1965									
Korea	34.34	5.80	13.54	15.53	23.32	41.81	38.85	7.21	2.16
Philippines	51.32	3.50	12.50	8.00	20.00	56.00	20.50	16.00	3.50
1988									
Korea	33.64	7.39	12.29	16.27	21.81	42.24	38.08	5.72	2.15
Philippines	45.73	5.20	9.10	13.30	19.90	52.50	33.20	10.10	3.67

Source: Benabou (1996).

An interesting case study is that of South Korea and the Philippines during the past thirty years, discussed by Benabou (1996). In the early 1960s, these two countries looked quite similar with regard to major macroeconomic indicators (GDP per capita, investment per capita, average saving rates, etc.), although they differed in the degree of income inequality, as we can see in table 1. In the Philippines the ratio of the income share of the top 20 percent to the bottom 40 percent of the population was twice as large as in South Korea. Over the following thirty year period, fast growth in South Korea resulted in a five-fold increase of the output level, while that of the Philippines barely doubled. That is, contrary to what the standard argument predicts, the more unequal country grew more slowly.

(b) On the reverse causal relationship from growth to inequality, the conventional wisdom is that inequality should obey the so-called Kuznets hypothesis. Based on a cross-section regression of GNP per head and income distribution across a large number of countries, Kuznets (1955) found an inverted U-shaped relation between income inequality (measured by the Gini coefficient) and GNP per head. That is, the lowest and highest levels of GNP per head were associated with low

Table 2. *Wage inequality measured as the ratio of the wages of the top to the bottom decile*

	1970	1980	1990
Germany		2.5	2.5
United States	3.2	3.8	4.5
France	3.7	3.2	3.2
Italy		2.3	2.5
Japan		2.5	2.8
United Kingdom	2.5	2.6	3.3
Sweden	2.1	2.0	2.1

Source: Piketty (1996).

inequality, while middle levels were associated with high inequality. This result, though cross-sectional, suggested a pattern of inequality along the development process. The conjecture was that inequality should necessarily increase during the early stages of development (due to urbanization and industrialization) and decrease later on as industries would attract a large fraction of the rural labor force. And indeed, in the US the share of total wealth owned by the 10 percent richest households rose from 50 percent around 1770, to 70–80 percent around 1870, and then receded back to 50 percent in 1970.

Up to the 1970s Kuznets' prediction seemed to be validated by the experience not only of the US but also of most of the OECD. However, the downward trend in inequality experienced by these economies during the twentieth century has reversed sharply in recent times. In particular, the past fifteen years have witnessed a significant increase in wage inequality both *between* and *within* groups of workers with different levels of education, as shown by figure 1 and table 2 below.

The rise in inequality shows that, as industrialization goes on, it is not necessarily the case that the income

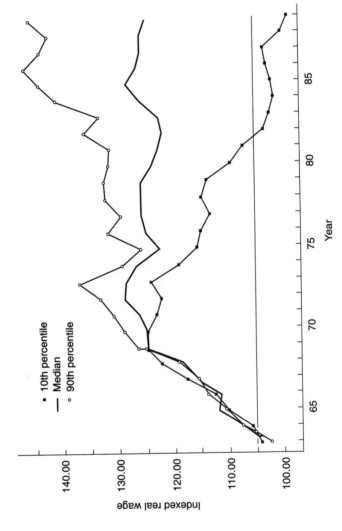

Figure 1 Indexed real weekly wages by percentile, 1963–1989
Source: Juhn, Murphy, and Pierce (1993).

and wage distributions should become less unequal. This suggests, in turn, that the evolution of inequality may be governed by factors other than the level of GNP per capita.

The aim of this first part of the book is to challenge the conventional wisdoms on inequality and growth which, as we have just argued, cannot explain recent empirical evidence. Our analysis remains within the framework of neoclassical economics. However, the introduction of additional aspects such as credit-market imperfections, moral hazard, non-neutral technical and organizational change, and labor-market institutions, gives a more complex and, we believe, more realistic picture of the relationship between inequality and economic growth. The first half of the lecture will be concerned with the effects of inequality on growth, with a view to providing new answers to the existing questions: Does inequality matter? If so, why is excessive inequality bad for aggregate growth? Is it possible to reconcile the above aggregate findings with existing microeconomic theories of incentives? In the second half, we will discuss the Kuznets' hypothesis. We will focus on the recent upsurge in wage and income inequality in developed countries and put forward candidate explanations for it, among which technological change will come out as the most important factor.

2 Inequality, incentives, and growth

Until recently, most economists agreed that inequality should, if at all, have a *stimulating* effect on capital accumulation and growth. Consequently, there would be a fundamental *tradeoff* between productive efficiency (and/or growth) and social justice, as redistribution would reduce differences in income and wealth, but would also diminish the incentives to accumulate wealth.

Two main considerations appear to underlie the presupposition that inequality should be growth enhancing. The first argument has to do with *investment indivisibilities*: investment projects, in particular the setting up of new industries or the implementation of innovations, often involve large sunk costs. In the absence of a broad and well-functioning market for shares, wealth obviously needs to be sufficiently concentrated in order for an individual (or a family) to be able to cover such large sunk costs and thereby initiate a new industrial activity. This issue has been recently emphasized by policy advisers to transition economies in Central and Eastern Europe and the former Soviet Union. Corporate governance is also subject to indivisibilities as a multiplicity of owners tends to complicate the decision-making process within the firm – when it is neces-sary to monitor the performance and effort of the firm's manager and employees, having many (dispersed) shareholders raises the scope for free-riding, resulting in a suboptimal level of monitoring.

The second argument, based on *incentive* considerations, was first formalized by Mirrlees (1971). Namely, in a moral hazard context where output realization depends on an *unobservable* effort borne by agents (or "employees"), rewarding the employees with a constant wage independent from (the observable) output performance, will obviously discourage them from investing any effort. On the other hand, making the reward too sensitive to output performance may also be inefficient from an *insurance* point of view when output realizations are highly uncertain and the employees are *risk averse.* This insurance argument is nothing but a natural way to formalize the social justice or "equity" motive for reducing inequality.

The basic incentive argument carries over to the aggregate economy when agents are identical and/or capital markets are perfect (see Rebelo 1991). Consider the neoclassical Ramsey–Cass–Koopmans growth model. Infinitely lived agents maximize their intertemporal utility subject to their budget con-straint. Each agent then solves the problem

$$\max_{c_t} \int_0^\infty u(c_t)\, e^{-\rho t} dt$$

subject to $w_t + r_t k_t = c_t$,

where ρ is the intertemporal discount rate, w_t the net wage, k_t the capital stock or wealth of the individual, c_t consumption, and r_t

the *after-tax* interest rate. Solving this program we obtain the optimal rate of growth of individual consumption as a function of the after-tax real interest rate

$$g = \frac{r - \rho}{\sigma},$$

where $\sigma = -u''(c)c/u'(c)$ is the intertemporal elasticity of substitution.

When all agents are identical, the above expression gives the aggregate rate of growth of the economy. Redistribution, by making the after-tax rate of interest smaller, reduces the return to saving, thus lowering the rate of growth of consumption and of capital accumulation.

We will now challenge, by means of a simple growth model, the conventional microeconomic tradeoff between equity and incentives. In particular, we will address whether such a tradeoff still exists when we introduce wealth heterogeneity or differences in human capital endowments across individuals together with *capital-market imperfections*. There are at least three reasons why redistribution to the less endowed can be growth enhancing when capital markets are imperfect:

(a) redistribution creates opportunities,
(b) redistribution improves borrowers' incentives,
(c) redistribution reduces macroeconomic volatility.

The next subsections examine under which conditions these mechanisms reverse the conventional tradeoff.

2.1 The opportunity-enhancing effect of redistribution

One of the cornerstones of neoclassical economics is the assumption that there are diminishing returns to capital. It is precisely this assumption that drives the familiar convergence results, both at the cross-country level (as in the Solow growth model) and for individuals (as in Tamura 1991). The convergence results rely crucially on perfect capital markets. However, as Stiglitz (1969) first pointed out, when there are decreasing returns to capital and capital markets are imperfect, individual wealth will not converge to a common level and the aggregate level of output will be affected by its distribution. This section reconsiders Stiglitz's arguments in the context of the recent literature on "endogenous growth."

For this purpose, we will consider a discrete-time version of the so-called AK growth model. This is a model in which, although there are diminishing returns to individual investments, there are constant returns to the aggregate capital stock,[1] so that the level of output can be expressed as $Y = AK$, where A is a constant and K the aggregate capital stock.[2]

There is only one good in the economy that serves both as a *capital* and *consumption* good. There is a continuum of overlapping-generations families, indexed by $i \epsilon [0,1]$. Each individual lives for two periods. The intertemporal utility of an individual i born at date t is given by

$$U_t^i = \ln c_t^i + \rho \cdot \ln d_t^i, \tag{1}$$

where c_t^i and d_t^i denote current and future consumption respectively. Individuals differ in their initial endowments of human capital. Let the endowment of individual i upon birth at date t be given by

$$w_t^i = \epsilon_t^i \cdot A_t,$$

where ϵ_t^i is an identically and independently distributed random shock that measures individual i's access to general knowledge. We normalize the mean of ϵ_t^i at one, so that $\int_0^1 w_t^i \, di = A_t.$

Individual i can either use the efficiency units of labor he is endowed with in order to produce the *current* consumption good, according to a linear "one-for-one" technology, or invest it into the production of the future consumption good. Production of the future consumption good (i.e., of the good

---

[1] See Aghion and Howitt (1998), chapter 1.
[2] The particular formulation we use in this subsection is taken from Benabou (1996).

available at date $(t+1)$) takes place at date t according to the AK technology

$$y_t^i = (k_t^i)^\alpha (A_t)^{1-\alpha}, \tag{2}$$

where k_t^i denotes the amount of investment by individual i at date t, A_t is the average level of human capital or knowledge available in period t, and $0 < \alpha < 1$.

We assume that the economy exhibits learning-by-doing: the more an economy produces in one period, the more it learns, and hence the greater the level of knowledge available in the next period. Formally

$$A_t = \int_0^1 y_{t-1}^i \, di = y_{t-1}. \tag{3}$$

That is, the accumulation of knowledge results from past production activities.

The interesting aspect of this section will result from the presence of heterogeneity or *inequality* among individuals of the same generation, and more specifically from the interplay between *capital-market imperfections* and the effect of *redistribution policies*.

The rate of growth between period $t-1$ and t is given by:

$$g_t = \ln \frac{y_t}{y_{t-1}}$$

that is

$$g_t = \ln \int_0^1 \left(\frac{k_t^i}{A_t} \right)^\alpha di,$$

where k_t^i is determined by intertemporal optimization. It then can be expressed simply as

$$g_t = \ln \frac{E_t(k^\alpha)}{A_t^\alpha},$$

where $E_t(k^\alpha)$ is the mathematical expectation over the output generated by individual investment levels k at date t.

Because of decreasing returns with respect to individual capital investments k^i (in other words, the fact that $\alpha < 1$ and therefore the function $k \to k^\alpha$ is concave) greater inequality between individual investments for a given aggregate capital stock will reduce aggregate output.[3] Therefore the more unequal the distribution of individual investments k_t^i, the smaller current aggregate output and therefore the lower the growth rate g in the above AK model.

Is this sufficient for redistribution to the less endowed to be growth enhancing? Not unless capital markets are imperfect. In the absence of capital-market imperfections all individuals choose to invest the same amount of capital $k^i \equiv k^*$, no matter what the initial distribution of human capital or "wealth" across individuals (see Aghion and Howitt 1998, chapter 9). The reason is that the opportunity cost of investing is the rate of interest, both for lenders and borrowers. Hence all individuals wish to invest up to the point where the marginal product of capital is equal to the rate of interest. Those whose wealth is above this level lend, those whose wealth is below it borrow. As a result, aggregate output and growth cannot be positively affected by wealth distribution policies.

Conversely, when capital markets are highly imperfect and therefore credit is scarce and costly, equilibrium investments under laissez-faire will remain unequal across individuals with heterogenous human-capital endowments. Consider the extreme situation in which borrowing is simply not possible and agents are constrained by their wealth, $k_t^i \leq w_t^i$. In this case, individual investments are simply a constant fraction of their wealth $k_t^i = s \cdot w_t^i$. Thus, in contrast to the perfect capital-market case, when credit is unavailable equilibrium investments will differ across individuals (being an increasing function of their initial endowments in human capital), and the rate of growth is given by the distribution of endowments

---

[3] This, in turn, follows from the following standard theorem in expected utility theory:

    Theorem: Let u be a concave function on the non-negative reals. Let X and Y be two random variables, such that the expectations $Eu(X)$ and $Eu(Y)$ exist and are finite, and such that Y is obtained from X through a sequence of mean-preserving spreads. Then $Eu(Y) \leq Eu(X)$. Because a convex function is the negative of a concave function, the opposite inequality holds for a convex function. Then, since

$$E_t(k^\alpha) = \int_0^\infty k^\alpha \cdot f_t(k) \, dk,$$

where $f_t(k)$ is the density function over individual investments at date t, $E_t(k^\alpha)$ is reduced by a mean-preserving spread.

$$g_t = \alpha \ln s + \ln \int_0^1 (\epsilon_t^i)^\alpha \, di.$$

More inequality is therefore bad for growth when capital markets are highly imperfect.

There is now a role for suitably designed redistribution policies in enhancing aggregate productive efficiency and growth. We will analyze the effects of an *ex-ante* redistribution of human-capital endowments. Consider a lump-sum transfer policy which consists of taxing highly endowed individuals directly on their endowments, and then using the revenues from this tax in order to subsidize human-capital improvements by the less endowed. Thus, the post-tax endowment of individual i can be simply defined by

$$\hat{w}_t^i = w_t^i + \beta(A - w_t^i), \quad 0 < \beta < 1. \tag{4}$$

Recall that A is the average endowment. Those with above-average wealth pay a tax of $\beta(w_t^i - A)$, while those with below-average receive a net subsidy, $\beta(A - w_t^i)$. Because it is a lump-sum tax it does not change the returns to k_t^i, and hence it only affects the incentives to invest in so far as it changes the current wealth of the individual. As the tax rate β increases and the distribution of disposable endowments becomes more equal across individuals, investments by the poorly endowed will increase while investments by the rich will decrease. However, as we already argued, because the production technology exhibits *decreasing* returns with respect to individual capital investments, we should expect redistribution to have an overall *positive* effect on aggregate output and growth. The rate of growth becomes:

$$g = \alpha \ln s + \ln \int_0^1 (\epsilon_t^i + \beta(1 - \epsilon_t^i))^\alpha di. \tag{5}$$

Now consider the term under the integral sign. As β increases, the heterogeneity among individual investment levels (which are proportional to $[\epsilon_t^i + \beta(1 - \epsilon_t^i)]$) decreases, and therefore so does the aggregate efficiency loss due to the unequal distribution of w^i. In the limiting case where $\beta = 1$, the term under the integral sign is constant across individuals i, and the highest possible growth rate is achieved.

The implication of the foregoing analysis is that, when credit is unavailable, redistribution to the poorly endowed, that is, to those individuals who exhibit the higher marginal returns to investment, will be growth enhancing.

2.2 The positive incentive effect of redistribution: questioning the traditional argument

Our modeling of capital-market imperfections in the previous subsection was somewhat extreme, as we were simply assuming away all possibilities of borrowing and lending. Using such a reduced-form representation of credit-market imperfections, we were able to show that redistributing wealth from the rich (whose marginal productivity of investment is relatively low, due to decreasing returns to individual capital investments) to the poor (whose marginal productivity of investment is relatively high, but who cannot invest more than their limited endowments w_i), would enhance aggregate productivity and therefore growth in the preceding AK model. In other words, *redistribution creates investment opportunities* in the absence of well-functioning capital markets, which in turn increases aggregate productivity and growth. Note that this "opportunity creation effect" of redistribution does not rely on incentive considerations: even if one could force the poor to invest *all* their initial endowments rather than maximize intertemporal utility as in the preceding analysis, redistributing wealth from the richest to the poorest individuals would still have an overall positive effect on aggregate productivity and growth, again because of decreasing returns to individual investments.

In this subsection we want to push the analysis one step further and introduce incentives as the microeconomic source of capital-market imperfections. This will enable us to challenge the view that the incentive effect of redistribution should always be negative. In fact, as we will now illustrate, *redistribution may sometimes be growth enhancing as a result of incentive effects only!*

Following Aghion and Bolton (1997), we introduce moral-hazard considerations as the explicit source of credit-market imperfections into the AK with overlapping-generations framework developed above. Specifically, we again assume the existence of a continuum of non-altruistic, overlapping-generations families, indexed by $i\epsilon[0,1]$. The utility of individual i in generation t is

$$U_t^i = d_t^i - c(e_t^i), \tag{6}$$

where d_t^i denotes individual i's second-period consumption (for simplicity we assume that individuals consume only when old), e^i is the non-monetary effort incurred by individual i when young, and $c(e^i) = A(e^i)^2/2$ denotes the non-monetary cost of effort. The parameter A still measures productivity on the current technology. As before, the human-capital endowment of individual i is taken to be an idiosyncratic proportion of average knowledge at date t, that is, $w_t^i = \epsilon_t^i \cdot A_t$.

The production technology involves an extreme form of U-shaped average cost curve with respect to capital investments, namely:

(a) the production activity requires a *fixed* and indivisible capital outlay equal to $k_t^i = \varphi \cdot A_t$;

(b) conditional upon the required investment $\varphi \cdot A_t$ being made at date t, the output from investment in this technology is uncertain and given by

$$y_t^i = \begin{cases} \sigma \cdot A_t \text{ with probability } e_t^i \\ 0 \text{ with probability } 1 - e_t^i, \end{cases}$$

where e_t^i is individual i's effort at date t. We assume that second-period outcomes y_t^i are independently identically distributed across individuals of the same generation.

The source of capital-market imperfection will be moral hazard with limited wealth constraints (or limited liability), in other words, the assumption that:

(a) efforts e^i are not observable;

(b) a borrower's repayment to his lenders cannot exceed his second period output y_t^i.

Consider the effort decision of an individual who does not need to borrow, that is, for whom $w^i \geq \varphi A$. The problem he faces is

$$\max_e \{e \cdot \sigma A - c(e)\},$$

which gives the first-best level of effort, $e^* = \sigma$.

An agent with initial endowment $w^i < \varphi A$ needs to borrow $b^i = \varphi A - w^i$ in order to invest. Let ρ be the unit repayment rate owed by individual w^i. Hence, he chooses effort e^i to maximize the expected second-period revenue net of both repayment to the lenders and effort cost, namely

$$e^i = \max_e \{e(\sigma A - \rho(\varphi \cdot A - w^i)) - c(e)\}$$

$$= e(\rho, w^i), \tag{7}$$

where $e(\rho, w^i) = \sigma - \rho(\varphi - w^i/A)$ is less than the first-best effort e^*, and is decreasing in ρ and increasing in w^i.

What is important in order to find moral hazard is that effort be increasing in the wealth of the individual. That is, for given ρ, the lower a borrower's initial wealth, the *less* effort he will devote to increasing the probability of success of his project. The more an individual needs to borrow in order to get production started, the less incentives he has to supply effort, in that he must share a larger fraction of the marginal returns from his effort with lenders. An immediate consequence of this result is that redistributing wealth toward borrowers will have a *positive* effect on their effort *incentives*. Whenever this positive incentive effect more than compensates the potentially negative incentive effect on lenders' efforts, then such a redistribution will indeed be growth enhancing based on incentive considerations only.

Before turning to the analysis of redistribution, let us make two important remarks. First, individuals with initial wealth $w^i \geq \varphi A$ (in other words the lenders), will systematically supply the first-best level of effort because they remain residual claimants on all returns from such effort: $e^i(w^i \geq \varphi A) = e^*$.

Second, when analyzing the relationship between initial wealth and effort, we have treated the repayment schedule ρ as given. However, because the risk of default on a loan increases with the size of the loan (the probability of success $e(\rho, w)$ decreases when *w* decreases), the unit repayment rate ρ may vary with *w* to reflect the change in default risk. Aghion and Bolton (1997) show that even once this effect is taken into account, effort is increasing in w^i.

The growth rate of the economy is given by

$$g = \ln \frac{\sigma A \cdot \int e^i di}{A}$$

$$= \ln \sigma + \ln \int_0^1 e^i di, \tag{8}$$

with efforts $e^i \leq \sigma$. If either (a) or (b) were violated, then the first-best effort would automatically be elicited from *all* individuals no matter what their human-capital endowments were. The growth rate would then be unaffected by redistribution and always be equal to $g = \ln \sigma^2$. This corresponds to nothing but the case of *perfect* capital markets, that is of capital markets that do *not* suffer from incentive problems. When there are incentive problems, the more unequal the distribution of wealth is, that is, the larger the number of individuals with wealth below the threshold level φA, the lower the aggregate level of effort will be. Consequently, inequality has a negative effect on both the income level and the growth rate.

We now have all the elements we need to analyze the incentive effects of redistribution. Because individuals with initial wealth $w^i \geq \varphi A$ supply the first-best effort $e^* = \sigma$, raising a lump-sum tax $t^i < w^i - \varphi A$ on the endowment of each such individual and then distributing the total proceeds among borrowers:

(i) will not affect the effort e^* supplied by the wealthy, whose *after-tax* endowments remain strictly above the required fixed cost φA;

(ii) will increase the effort supplied by any subsidized borrower.

The above redistribution scheme will then have an unambiguously positive *incentive* effect on growth, as efforts e^i either increase or remain constant as a result of redistribution.

We have just put the traditional incentive-distribution tradeoff upside-down, since we have shown that in the context of an imperfect credit market with moral hazard, redistribution enhances growth. For quite similar reasons inequality will tend to discourage cooperation between uneven equity holders engaged in the same venture or partnership. This lack of cooperation may typically take the form of *free-riding* by the poor on the rich's effort.[4] The effect on (long-run) growth will obviously be negative.

To see how inequality induces free-riding consider the following set up. Suppose that the economy gives birth to only two individuals each period, and that these two individuals (who both live for two periods) need to join forces (that is, to pool their initial resources) in order to produce. Let $\bar{w}_t = \bar{w}A_t$ and $w_t = wA_t$ denote the initial endowment of the richer and the poorer of these two individuals. As above, we denote by $\varphi \cdot A_t$ the fixed cost of the project initiated at date t, and we assume that

$$\bar{w} + \underline{w} \geq \varphi > \bar{w} > \underline{w}.$$

In other words, the project requires the financial participation of both individuals in order to be implemented at all.

Once the fixed cost φA_t has been sunk, the project yields $\sigma \cdot A_t$ with probability $(\bar{e} + \underline{e})/2$ and zero with probability $(1 - \bar{e} + \underline{e})/2)$, where $\bar{e}$ and $\underline{e}$ denote the effort of the richer and the poorer individuals. The return of the project is then distributed between the two individuals according to their shares in the total investment. They can choose whether to exert one unit of effort or no effort at all. There is a "moral hazard in team" problem between the two individuals.

Suppose that there is a non-zero effort cost for each individual, and let us assume, as before, that individuals only care for expected second-period output net of their effort cost. Then, the resulting Nash equilibrium depends on the degree of inequality. In particular, when the discrepancy between the rich and the poor is sufficiently large relative to the cost of effort, full cooperation between both individuals (i.e., $\bar{e} = \underline{e} = 1$) will not be sustainable in equilibrium. Rather, the poor individual will free-ride on

---

[4] Legros and Newman (1994) have also emphasized the idea that a high degree of inequality between the rich and the poor may induce the rich to choose inefficient organizational structures in order to better take advantage of their bargaining power *vis-à-vis* poor partners within the same firms.

Table 3. *Income inequality is increased by high macroeconomic volatility*

	Index of inequality	Percentage of difference
Income inequality		
Latin America	6.284	
Industrial countries	*2.270*	
Difference	4.014	100.0
Impact of		
Initial income inequality	2.047	51.0
Growth in per capita income	0.067	1.7
Average inflation	0.029	0.7
Volatility of real GDP	0.912	22.7
Unexplained	0.959	23.9

Source: Gavin and Hausman (1996b).

the rich one, as part of the (unique) equilibrium $\bar{e} = 1, \underline{e} = 0$. Moving toward a more egalitarian distribution of wealth (i.e., toward $\bar{w} = \underline{w} = 1/2$) between the two individuals, will favor their cooperation and thereby increase the level of output and the growth rate.

2.3 Macroeconomic volatility

Another reason why excessive inequality may be bad for growth is that it generates macroeconomic volatility. The idea that macro-economic instability is fundamentally detrimental to growth has been pointed out by various authors, especially Alesina and Perotti (1996). It also emerges quite clearly from the cross-country regression for Latin America performed by Hausmann and Gavin (1996a,b). Interestingly for our purpose in this chapter, Hausmann and Gavin find (a) a *positive* correlation between macroeconomic volatility and both income inequality and finan-cial underdevelopment (table 3), and (b) a *negative* correlation between volatility and growth (figure 2).

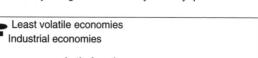

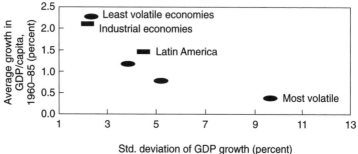

Figure 2 Volatility and growth of real GDP per capita
Source: Gavin and Haussman (1996)

Several explanations have been put forward to account for the correlation between [high] inequality and macroeconomic volatility. Alesina and Perotti (1996) maintain that causality runs from high inequality to political and institutional instability, which in turn results in macroeconomic volatility. The approach we take in this subsection, based on Aghion, Banerjee, and Piketty (1997) (ABP from now onwards), postulates a direct effect of inequality on macroeconomic fluctuations. Inequality, however, takes the form of unequal access to investment opportunities across individuals, which, together with a high degree of capital-market imperfection, can generate persistent credit cycles. Beyond its theoretical appeal, we believe that the ABP set-up summarized below can be useful in understanding the kind of financial crises recently experienced by the growing economies of South-East Asia.

Specifically we consider a dynamic economy in which only a fraction of the active population has access to high-yield investment opportunities. There are a number of reasons why access to investment opportunities may be restricted. Particular skills, ideas, or connections may be required, and often there may be crucial information that can only be acquired by those already in the business. Investment indivisibilities are another potential cause. Individuals may also differ in their attitudes toward risk, hence only those with little risk aversion will be willing to undertake risky projects rather than work under a riskless employment contract. It is this inequality of access to investments and the consequent separation of investors and savers that will give rise to volatility.

Consider an economy where there are two production technologies: a traditional technology and a high-yield technology. Two crucial assumptions are needed for inequality to affect volatility:

1 Inequality of access to investment: Only a fraction of savers can directly invest in high-yield projects, whereas all individuals can invest in the low-yield technology.

2 Credit-market imperfections: Because of incentive compatibility considerations, an investor with wealth w can borrow only a limited amount, vw, where $v < \infty$.

Now assume that all individuals in the economy save a constant fraction of their wealth, s. What do the saving and the investment functions look like? The total supply of funds in period t is a fraction s of the aggregate level of wealth in period $t-1$. Savings at t are therefore independent of any variable in that period. The total demand for investment in the high-return project at time t is proportional to the wealth of those who have access to the high-yield investment, and thus is also completely determined by the previous period's income and by the (exogenously given) credit multiplier. There is therefore no market-clearing mechanism that will equalize the supply of funds and the demand for investment in the more productive technology. Consequently the economy will experience either "idle" savings (i.e., a fraction of savings are not invested in high-yield projects) or unrealized investment opportunities.

The link between inequality and volatility hence stems from the fact that those who invest and those who save are not the same individuals. Slumps are periods of idle savings, in which funds are invested in the low-return technology therefore generating a loss of potential output. If everybody had the possibility of investing in the high-yield technology, all agents would choose to invest all their savings, and there would be no slumps. Similarly, if investors were not credit constrained they could absorb all savings.

More precisely, during booms investors' net wealth increases and therefore so does their borrowing capacity, vw. Investors can thus accumulate debt during booms, thereby increasing the demand for investable funds. The interest rate is given by the marginal product of capital. Since all funds are invested in the high-yield technology, interest rates are high during booms. Eventually, the accelerated increase in their debt repayment obligations ends up squeezing the investors' borrowing capacity, up to a point where a positive fraction of savings becomes idle. At this point the economy experiences a slump: some funds have to be invested in the traditional technology, therefore the marginal product of capital falls and interest rates drop. This in turn allows the investors to progressively reconstitute their borrowing capacity, and so eventually the economy will re-enter a boom. If the fraction of the population with high-yield investment possibilities is small enough and/or the credit multiplier low enough, there will be continuous oscillations of the investment level. Such volatility of investment in turn implies that there are unexploited production possibilities and hence the long-run growth rate is lower than it could be.

The government has two structural policy options to try to move the economy out of the above cyclical equilibrium into a situation in which all savings are invested in the high-return production technology. One is to reduce the borrowing constraints, thus increasing the credit multiplier and ensuring that there is sufficient demand for funds. This is, however, a hard policy to implement unless the government is willing to lend to individuals itself. Moreover, if the credit constraint is the result of a moral hazard problem, such as that examined in subsection 2.2, it would not be possible to increase the credit multiplier without generating adverse incentive effects. A second structural policy consists in reducing the degree of inequality of access to investment. By increasing the fraction of savers that can directly invest in high-yield projects, the economy can move to a permanent-boom situation and thus increase its growth rate. Structural reforms such as investing in infrastructure or in human capital, or reducing the bureaucratic obstacles faced by entrepreneurs that wish to set up a firm, would reduce entry barriers and promote growth.

Structural policies may be hard to implement though, especially in the short run. An alternative would be to transfer the idle funds from savers to investors. This policy ensures that all savings are invested in the high-yield technology. However, it transfers resources from those that are worse off to those that are better off. Yet ABP show that this policy does not entail negative distributive consequences for savers. The higher level of income trickles down to savers for two reasons: first, the interest rate is higher, so (poor) lenders are better off; second, as more capital is invested in the high-yield technology, the productivity of labor and thus the wage rate is also higher.

Our analysis so far has concentrated on the case of a closed economy and much of the output cycle appeared to be driven by movements in the real interest rate. However, in more recent work with P. Bacchetta and A. Banerjee, we are considering a small open economy extension of the same framework, where real interest rates remain fixed at the international market-clearing level and the transmission variable becomes the price of non-tradeable goods in terms of the tradeable good. More precisely, high-yield investments in the domestic economy require the use of non-tradeable goods (such as real estate) as inputs to produce tradeable goods. Then, the story goes as follows: during a boom the domestic demand for non-tradeable goods keeps going up as high-yield investments build up, and thus so does the price of non-tradeables relative to that of tradeables. This, together with the accumulation of debt that still goes on during booms, will eventually squeeze investors' borrowing capacity and therefore the demand for non-tradeable goods. At this point, the economy experiences a slump and two things occur: the price of non-tradeables collapses to the level where it is equal to the real rate of return of the asset (i.e., it falls relative to that of tradeables), while a fraction of the assets on offer is not purchased as there are not enough investment funds. This second effect has real consequences, as those individuals who cannot undertake tradeable production have to move into the backyard technology. The collapse in the price of non-tradeables thus results in a contraction of the tradeable-goods sector and of the level of real output.

Unlike in Krugman (1998), the argument that we have just presented does not rely on any regime or policy change.[5] Investors are constrained in their borrowing at any point in time. The increase in the price of non-tradeable goods relative to tradeables and the accumulation of debt, make the credit-market constraint bind at a certain moment in time, and bring about the collapse in the price of non-tradeables. The effect of credit-market imperfections would, clearly, be worsened if production were risky and if there were moral hazard on the part of investors. What is new about this approach is that the financial slump is the consequence of rapid growth. Growth is financed by the accumulation of debt. The debt build up and the consequent increase in the price of non-tradeables is what causes the crisis. This raises the question of what is sustainable growth. If periods of fast growth are followed by slumps due to excessive debt build-up, it may be a better long-run strategy to allow the economy to develop at a slower but steady pace.

2.4 Political economy

Economic conflicts surface through the political process, especially when the society as a whole must decide about redistribution or public-good investments such as education or health. By affecting the outcome of the political game, inequality will directly influence the extent of redistribution and thereby the rate of growth. Interestingly, the *direction* in which inequality affects growth through the political process turns out to depend heavily on the importance of credit constraints, as we will now illustrate.

As has been argued in the previous subsections, redistribution affects the rate of growth in an AK-model. If inequality determines the extent of redistribution, it will then have an indirect effect on the rate of growth of the economy. Several authors, such

---

[5] Krugman (1998) argues that the Asian crisis has been caused by moral hazard on the part of financial intermediaries whose liabilities were guaranteed by the government. The resulting overinvestment and excessive risk-taking made asset prices rise. Eventually, a "change in regime" has implied that liabilities are no longer guaranteed and asset prices have collapsed.

as Alesina and Rodrik (1994), Persson and Tabellini (1994), and Benabou (1996), maintain that inequality affects taxation through the political process when individuals are allowed to vote in order to choose the tax rate (or, equivalently, vote to elect a government whose program includes a certain redistributive policy). In general, we would expect that in very unequal societies, a majority of voters prefer high redistribution than in more equal societies. If redistribution is harmful for growth, then more unequal societies would grow faster.

To illustrate this argument suppose that individuals are, as before, endowed with different amounts of human capital, given by $w_t^i = \epsilon_t^i \cdot A_t$, and that production of the future consumption good takes place according to the AK-technology. The government now introduces redistributive taxation that takes the following form: there is a proportional tax on individual investments and the revenue is used to distribute a lump-sum subsidy which is proportional to the average investment. This is, an individual i with pre-tax investment k^i ends up with the post-tax investment

$$k^i(\tau) = (1-\tau) \cdot k^i + \tau \cdot k, \quad 0 < \tau < 1,$$

where k is the average investment. Clearly, those with above-average investments pay a net tax, while those with below-average k_i receive a net subsidy.

When capital markets are perfect so that all agents can borrow at the risk-free interest rate, all individuals choose to invest the same amount $k^i = s(\tau) \cdot w$, where $s(\tau)$ is the saving rate. Individual investments depend on the *average* endowment and on the saving rate. In the absence of moral hazard, the saving rate is the same for all individuals and is decreasing in the tax rate due to the standard negative incentive effect (see appendix 2). Moreover, in the AK-model, the growth rate is a function of the saving rate, $g_t = \alpha \ln s(\tau)$. The standard incentive argument then implies that a high tax rate, by reducing the net return to investment, reduces the fraction of wealth that is invested and the growth rate.

The tax rate affects individuals differently depending on their initial income, as it has two distinct effects: on the one hand, it affects an agent's current income through the net tax/subsidy; on the other hand, it affects his future income through the changes in the growth rate. In fact, we can express the indirect utility function of individual i as a function of his relative wealth and the tax rate

$$U^i(\tau) = V(\tau) + G(w^i/w, \tau).$$

The term $V(\tau)$ captures the *incentive* effect of redistribution and is the same for all agents: redistribution affects the growth rate and hence utility. In our particular example, $V(\tau)$ is decreasing in τ as a result of the negative incentive effect. $G(w^i/w, \tau)$ is an individual-specific term that reflects the *redistribution* effect of the tax. Those agents with wealth above w pay a net tax, as they are taxed more than they receive in subsidies. Hence for them the term $G(w^i/w, \tau)$ is negative. For those agents with $w^i < w$, this term is positive as they receive a net subsidy. The net investment of the individual with average wealth, $w^i = w$, is unaffected by the tax, i.e., $G(1, \tau)$ is zero. Moreover, the impact of an increase in the tax rate on $G(w^i/w, \tau)$ depends on the relative income position of the individual: a higher tax reduces the utility of agents with above-average wealth through the redistribution effect, and increases that of agents with below-average w^i. We have

$$\frac{\partial G(w^i/w, \tau)}{\partial \tau} \begin{cases} < 0 \text{ for } w^i > w \\ = 0 \text{ for } w^i = w \\ > 0 \text{ for } w^i < w. \end{cases}$$

An individual will prefer the tax rate at which the marginal increase in utility of redistribution equals the marginal loss due to the incentive effect. The preferred tax rate of individual i is given by the first-order condition $\partial U^i(\tau)/\partial \tau = 0$

$$\frac{\partial V(\tau)}{\partial \tau} = -\frac{\partial G(w^i/w, \tau)}{\partial \tau}.$$

Individuals with initial wealth equal to w or greater will prefer a zero tax rate, as a higher tax reduces their utility through both the incentive effect and the redistribution effect. Individuals with initial wealth $w^i < w$ will prefer a positive tax rate $\tau(w^i)$. The resulting preferred tax rate $\tau(w^i)$ is decreasing in w^i. Not surprisingly, poorer individuals will prefer a higher tax rate τ^i, as the redistribution effect is stronger the lower w^i.

Assume now that the tax rate is endogenously determined each period through majority voting. Given that the intertemporal utilities $U^i(\tau)$ are single-peaked for $w^i < w$, the equilibrium tax rate τ will be that chosen by the median voter. Inequality therefore affects the degree of redistribution: the higher the degree of wealth equality, as measured by the ratio of the median voter's wealth to average wealth, the higher the tax rate τ will be. Hence *in the absence of credit-market imperfections, more inequality* (in the sense of a lower ratio of median to average wealth) *will lead to more redistribution and therefore to lower growth.*

As we noted above, appreciating the effect of capital-market imperfections is crucial to understanding the relationship between inequality and growth. Is the result that greater inequality is harmful for growth robust to the introduction of capital-market imperfections? To address this question we should couple the political economy arguments just presented with the models developed in previous subsections. Consider, in particular, the opportunity-creation effect. Suppose that a lump-sum tax β is introduced, and that the tax rate is chosen by majority voting. As we already argued in subsection 2.1, this tax has no incentive effect. It, however, affects the individual's utility in two ways. There is a redistribution effect, that implies that those with wealth below average benefit from redistribution, those with average wealth are unaffected, while individuals for whom $w^i > w$ experience a reduction in their net wealth. There is a second effect that reflects the aggregate loss from investment inequality, which arises in the no credit-market case. This loss is itself a consequence of the assumption of decreasing returns to individual capital investments; to the extent that it affects aggregate knowledge A at any point in time, this cost of inequality is to be borne by *all* individuals, the poor *and* the rich, in the economy. In terms of the indirect utility function, $U^i(\tau) = V(\tau) + G(w^i/w,\tau)$, this means that now $V(\tau)$ is increasing in the tax rate. In particular, the individual with average wealth w will now vote for a positive tax rate because (1) the redistribution effect leaves his wealth unchanged, and (2) redistribution creates investment opportunities, increasing aggregate knowledge and therefore his income. The larger the degree of inequality, the more the median voter will benefit from the direct redistribution effect, and the higher his preferred tax rate will be. The overall impact of greater inequality on the growth rate is now ambiguous: on the one hand, it reduces growth, as seen in subsection 2.1, on the other, it results in a greater degree of redistribution and therefore faster growth.

A similar point is made by Saint-Paul and Verdier (1993), Glomm and Ravikumar (1992), and Perotti (1993) who analyze the voting process over public education spending aimed at circumventing wealth constraints on private education investments. In these papers redistribution takes the form of public education or education subsidies, while revenue is raised through a tax on the returns to investment. Consequently, redistribution has both a negative incentive effect and a positive *opportunity creation* effect. The rate of growth, and hence the term $V(\tau)$ in the indirect utility function, are a nonmonotonic function of the tax rate. When inequality is great, so that a large fraction of the population is constrained in their investments, the opportunity creation effect dominates; for more equal distributions, public education only slightly increases the number of agents that have access to education while it reduces the investment of a large part of the population through the incentive effect, resulting in a reduction in the growth rate. Since the tax rate is strictly increasing in the degree of inequality, the resulting relationship between wealth distribution and growth is U-shaped.

2.5 Discussion

The main conclusion we can draw from this section is that when we allow for heterogeneity among agents along with capital-market imperfections, the traditional argument that inequality has a positive impact on growth is strongly challenged. Consider, for example, the opportunity-enhancing effect. Our argument relies on three assumptions: first, that agents are heterogenous; second, that capital markets are highly imperfect; third, that the production technology exhibits diminishing returns to capital. These may look quite strong. However, there is, at least, one particular type of investment for which these assumptions clearly hold: education.[6] Investments in human capital are characterized by strong diminishing returns. Moreover, borrowing in order to make such an intangible investment is usually expensive (if not impossible) and hence family wealth becomes a major determinant of the size of the investment. If we view k_t^i as an investment in education and g as the rate of growth of human capital (which in turn determines the rate of output growth, as argued by Lucas (1988)), then our analysis predicts a negative relationship between wealth inequality and the rate of growth.

The importance of moral hazard in determining individual actions is well-known, and subsection 2.2 has examined its consequences for the aggregate level of investment. We saw how a lump-sum tax and transfer system results in faster growth. Consider now a transfer system in which revenue is raised through distortionary (*ex-post*) taxation. In this case there are two incentive effects: the standard effect whereby taxation reduces net returns and hence lenders' incentive to invest, and moral hazard with wealth constraints which decreases the effort exerted by entrepreneurs whose projects are largely financed by borrowing. Whether redistribution increases or decreases the rate of growth then depends on whether the standard effect of taxes on those with high wealth is smaller or greater than the positive impact on the effort of those with low wealth levels.

The third aspect we have dealt with introduces a different, and much neglected, concept of inequality. It is not the distribution of wealth that we look at, but rather the social and institutional environment that affects access to investment projects. As we have seen, this institutional source of inequality will affect both the distribution of wealth and the rate of growth of the economy.

Overall, inequality actually proves *bad* for growth in several circumstances. Redistribution is then growth enhancing because it creates opportunities, improves borrowers' incentives and/or because it reduces macroeconomic volatility. In such instances, there is no longer a tradeoff between equity and efficiency goals, and policies designed to tackle one then have a

---

[6] A growing literature addresses how inequality affects growth through the possibilities of agents to invest in education. See Saint-Paul and Verdier (1993), Galor and Zeira (1993), Perotti (1993), and García-Peñalosa (1995).

positive impact on the other. If reducing inequality can foster growth, an important question arises: is there any virtuous circle, that is, does economic development bring about a steady decrease in inequality which in turn increases income levels? We will see in the next section that this has not been the case in OECD economies over the past twenty years. As the process of development has gone on, income inequality has been pushed up by several factors, among which technical change has played a major role.

3 Technical change and the Kuznets' hypothesis

General interest into questions of how technical change and growth affect inequality has been revived in the last few years by new empirical evidence questioning the relevance of the so-called Kuznets' hypothesis. According to this traditional view of the development process, in the long run growth is bound to bring about a steady reduction in inequality.

However, recent empirical studies (e.g., Juhn, Murphy, and Pierce, 1993; Machin, 1996) have pointed to a substantial increase in wage and income inequality in several OECD countries during the past twenty years.[7] This has been the case in Australia, Austria, Belgium, and Japan, with the biggest rise taking place by some distance in the UK and North America. The ratio of the 90th to the 10th percentile of the male wage distribution rose from 2.53 to 3.21 in the UK between 1980 and 1990 and from 4.76 to 5.63 in the US over 1980–1989.[8] The increase in income inequality is largely due to changes in the wage component.[9] These changes can in turn be decomposed into four elements:

(a) an increase in *educational* wage differentials, that is, in wage inequality across different educational cohorts. Between 1979 and 1988, the wage ratio of university graduates to workers with no qualification increased

---

[7] See Atkinson (1996) and Piketty (1996) for illuminating surveys of the relevant empirical and theoretical literature on the determinants of income and wage inequality.   [8] See OECD Employment Outlook (1993).

[9] See Atkinson (1996), pp. 4 and 12 and figure 1.

from 1.53 to 1.65 in the UK, and the ratio of college to high school graduates rose from 1.37 to 1.51 in the US.[10]

(b) an increase in *occupational* wage differentials. The non-manual/manual worker earnings ratio displays a similar pattern to changes in the educational premium. It rose by 7 percent in the US and 14 percent in the UK during the 1980s.

(c) an increase in *age related* wage differentials.[11] The 45–49/20–24 year old wage ratio rose from 1.27 to 1.36 in the UK between 1974 and 1990 and from 1.76 to 2.4 in the US over 1970–1990.

(d) an increase in *within-group* wage inequality, that is inequality which is not accounted for by the above between-group changes. Figures 3 and 4 below (from Juhn, Murphy, and Pierce (1993)) present evidence of an increase in wage inequality *within* educational or experience groups in the US. They look at the logarithm of wage changes for workers in different percentiles of the various groups' wage distributions. Figure 3 separates workers with 1–10 years of work experience from those with 21–30 years, while figure 4 divides workers into two groups according to their education attainment. If there had been no increase in wage inequality within educational groups and age cohorts, the two curves on each of these figures would be horizontal.

Further evidence is provided by Machin (1996) who looks at the residual standard deviation obtained when estimating simple human-capital equations where earnings are treated as a function of age (and its square) and the number of years of schooling. His estimates on British and American data yield similar results: the residual standard deviation in real hourly earnings has increased by 14 percent in the US between 1979 and 1991 and by 23 percent in the UK between 1979 and 1993.

Various explanations have been offered for this observed upsurge of inequality in developed countries. However, the evidence

[10] See Machin (1996).   [11] See Machin (1996).

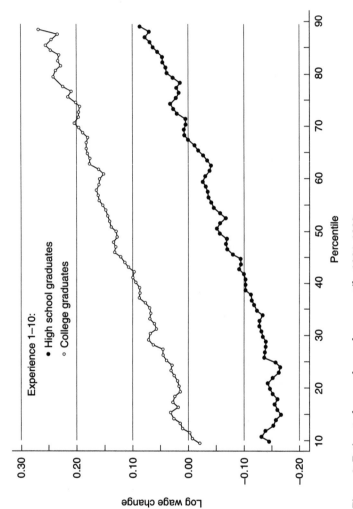

Figure 3 Estimated wage change by percentile, 1964–1988

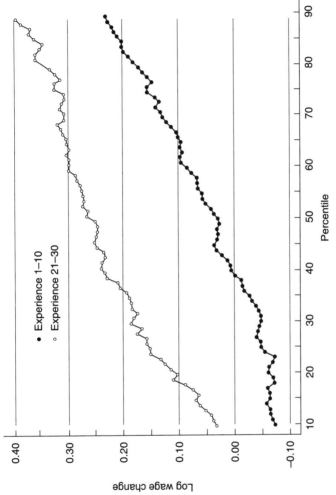

Figure 4 Estimated wage change by percentile, 1964–1988

on both the importance of the *wage component* in the measured increase in income inequality *and* the *episodic nature* of inequality changes during the past fifty years, leads us to believe that a major cause of these changes has been a shift in the relative demands for skilled and unskilled labor. And indeed, writes Atkinson, "there appears to be widespread agreement on the fact that there has been a shift in demand away from unskilled labor in favor of skilled workers,"[12] and that this provides a straightforward explanation for rising earnings dispersion.

Three competing explanations have been proposed for this structural change in the relative demand for skilled labor: the *impact of trade* with the rapidly growing East Asian economies, *skill-biased technological change*, and *organizational change*. Moreover, the weakening of *labor-market institutions* seems to have played an important role in the upsurge of wage inequality, although it does not entail any demand shift. The purpose of this section is to examine the validity of these various explanations.

Our analysis will be organized as follows. Subsection 3.1 evaluates the trade hypothesis, and discusses a growing empirical literature that has tried to sort out how much of the observed rise in the skill premium can be explained by trade versus skill-biased technical change. These studies claim to present evidence that trade can only explain a small fraction of the change in wage inequality. However, we argue that they neglect aspects that would magnify the impact of trade, such as the role of imports as intermediate production factors. Subsection 3.2 considers the role of skill-biased technical change as a possible explanation for the observed behavior of the skill differential. First, in subsection 3.2.1, we analyze the effect of *disembodied technical change*, and in particular we argue that the acceleration in the diffusion of new technologies can result in episodes of increasing wage inequality across skill groups. We then reconsider the trade hypothesis under skill-biased technical change and show that it can account for a steady rise in wage inequality across educational groups. Subsection 3.2.2 focuses on *embodied technical change*. It examines what features of the aggregate production function result in

---

[12] See Atkinson (1996).

skill-biased embodied technical progress and reports empirical estimates of the relevant parameters. We then introduce learning-by-doing and intersectoral mobility considerations to provide an explanation for the observed increase in wage inequality *within* education groups during the past twenty-five years.

Finally, what about the evolutions in the relative *supply* of unskilled and skilled labor? As a follow up of our discussion of the role of trade liberalization and skill-biased technical change on relative labour demands, we consider whether systematic supply-side forces will offset or reinforce demand-side forces. In particular, we are interested in:

(a) the extent to which an increase in the skill premium should encourage *education spending* (both public and private). Since education in turn increases the relative supply of skilled labor, can this policy reverse, or at least slow down, the trend in wage inequality? (see subsection 3.2.2.d),

(b) the role that *labor-market institutions* may have played in the increase in wage inequality (see subsection 3.3),

(c) the impact that changes in the *internal organization of firms* have had on the productivity gap between individuals with different skills or experience (see subsection 3.4).

3.1 International trade

The argument that trade is responsible for the increase in wage inequality stems largely from Heckscher–Ohlin theory (see in particular Krugman 1995). According to it, countries specialize in the production of those commodities which use intensively the factors of production they are abundantly endowed with. Developing countries that are abundant in unskilled labor but scarce in skilled labor tend to export goods (including material inputs) that are intensive in unskilled labor. Skill-abundant countries export computer software and import more primary inputs. Under such specialization conditions, a globalization boom causes predictable inequality trends. In the poor country – where unskilled labor (at the bottom of the earnings distribution) is cheap and skilled labor (at the top of the earnings distribution) is expensive – the trade boom drives up the demand for unskilled labor and drives down the demand for skilled labor, thus erasing some earnings inequality. In the rich country – where (at least relative to the poor country) unskilled labor is expensive and skilled labor cheap – the trade boom drives up the demand for skilled labor and drives down the demand for unskilled labor. If wages are flexible, such shifts in demand would create more earnings inequality.[13] Alternatively, if the wage of unskilled labor is to some extent rigid, the fall in the relative demand for unskilled labor would manifest itself in a rise in unskilled unemployment.[14]

The argument is best illustrated with the aid of a simple figure, taken from Wood and Ridao-Cano (1996). Suppose there are two production factors: skilled labor and unskilled labor. There is a large number of goods of different skill intensities. Now consider two countries. Country A has a lower relative endowment of skilled labor than country B. Figure 5 depicts the relationship between the ratio of the skilled to the unskilled wage, denoted ω, and the relative labor supply or fraction of the labor force that has skills, denoted s. The given skill ratios are represented by the two vertical lines, where S_1 is the supply of skills in country A and S_2 that in country B.

When the two countries start trading, the skill-rich economy will experience an increase in the price of skill-intensive commodities, and hence an increase in the relative demand for skilled labor. Similarly, country A will experience an increase in the price of the labor-intensive goods and a reduction in the demand for skills. That is, the demand curve becomes flatter, represented by

[13] Whether these trade effects are big or small is an empirical issue, but note that there is no reason why they should be correlated with "development." This example has been greatly simplified by considering only two classes of labor and earnings distribution, but the story can be elaborated to confront income distribution by adding land and landlords (at the top of the distribution) and capital and capitalists (near the top of the distribution).

[14] In the US and UK, the 1980s saw a large rise in the relative wage of skilled workers, while in a number of other OECD countries unskilled unemployment rates rose relative to skilled. See, for instance, Katz and Murphy (1992), Murphy and Welch (1992), Wood (1994), and Nickell and Bell (1995).

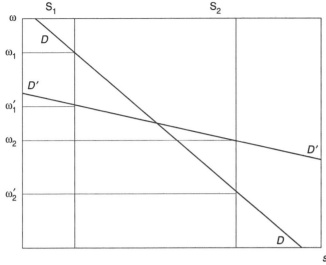

Figure 5

the D'D' line. This change in demand results in a higher skill premium in country B and a lower skill premium in country A than under autarchy.

Rapid growth in East Asia in the past two decades has been associated with an increase in exports of goods intensive in unskilled labor, and (to some degree, although this is partly a point of debate) a fall in the price of those exports. Conventional trade theory then predicts that this would cause the rise in skilled wage differentials observed in developed countries. A growing empirical literature has tried to sort out how much of this rise can be explained by technical change versus trade with newly industrializing countries. Trade between high-skill and low-skill economies should cause, in the former, an increase in the demand for (domestic) skill-intensive commodities at the expense of the demand for domestic unskilled-intensive commodities (which directly face competition from the developing south). This, in turn, would induce a reallocation of labor from low-skill to high-skill industries in skill-abundant countries. In contrast, skill-biased technical change would induce a shift in labor demand toward skilled labor *within* all industries.

Berman, Bound, and Griliches (1994) distinguish the impact of technical progress from that of changes in product demand – driven by trade liberalization – by decomposing the variations in the share of white-collar workers in employment.[15] Assume that $E_i = X_i/N_i$ is the share of white-collar workers X in total employment (N) of industry i. $S_i = N_i/N$ is the share of industry i's employment in total manufacturing employment N. Then

$$\Delta E = \sum_{i=1}^{N} \Delta S_i \bar{E}_i + \sum_{i=1}^{N} \Delta E_i \bar{S}_i,$$

where ΔE is the aggregate change in the share of white-collar workers. The first term reflects changes in the share of employment *between* industries, as caused by an increase in the relative demand addressed to white-collar-intensive industries. The second term captures the *within-industry* component, that is, skill upgrading due to skill-biased, blue-collar labor-saving technical progress.

The within component is, by far, the most important one. It accounts for 70 percent of the rise in the white-collar share in employment in the US, between 1979 and 1987. Using a similar method for the UK between 1979 and 1990, Machin (1995) reports that 82 percent of the increase in the non-manual share is due to within-industry shifts. Hence, only a minor part of the shift away from manual/blue-collar workers to non-manual/white-collars is due to between-industry changes.[16]

Whilst the above-mentioned evidence points to skill-biased

---

[15] This blue-/white-collar distinction proves to be highly correlated with a high-school/college educational classification. In the US, in 1987, only 17 percent of blue-collar workers had more than a high-school education, as opposed to 35 percent of clerical workers, 70 percent of sales workers, and 78 percent of managers and professionals. The same pattern holds for the UK (Machin, 1995) with a correlation coefficient of 0.631 between the share of non-manual workers and the share of workers with a degree.

[16] Several other studies arrive at similar conclusions. For instance Borjas, Freeman, and Katz (1992) obtain that a maximum of 15 percent of the growth of the college-non-college wage differential in the US is due to imports. Lawrence and Slaughter (1993) find little evidence that the relative prices of less-skill-intensive goods have fallen in the United States, as the trade arguments would require (see also Sachs and Shatz 1994). Krugman (1995) summarizes this research as indicating that the effect of East Asian imports on industrialized countries' labor markets has been small, although its impact cannot be neglected.

technical change as an unavoidable part of the wage inequality story, the fact that the shift in labor demand toward skilled labor has taken place within both traded *and* non-traded goods sectors does not suffice, however, to totally disregard trade liberalization when trying to explain the observed increase in wage inequality between skilled and unskilled labor. The above argument relies on the assumption that traded goods are primarily final goods, and, consequently, trade liberalization would have the effect of shifting demand from unskilled-intensive to skill-intensive goods. If, on the other hand, traded goods were mainly *inputs* into further production, the implications would be very different. A lower price of intermediaries would shift the demands for other inputs, increasing that of complementary production factors and reducing the demand for substitutes. When unskilled labor is more substitutable for physical inputs than skilled labor is, cheap physical inputs increase the relative demand for skilled workers, shifting the within-industry labor demands in all industries that use such inputs, irrespective of whether they themselves produce traded or untraded goods and of whether they are skill- or unskilled-labor intensive. Consequently, because there is no shift in the demand for final goods, one cannot interpret the evidence of an absence of between-industry shifts as refuting the role of trade.

An interesting Ph.D. thesis recently produced by Bertrand Koebel from the Louis Pasteur University of Strasbourg, may help reconcile the *skill-biased technical change* and *trade liberalization explanations*. Koebel (1997) and Falk and Koebel (1997) show evidence of a substantial degree of *substitutability between material inputs and unskilled labor* in the manufacturing and construction sectors in Germany. Trade liberalization that reduces the price of material inputs would, then, have the effect of shifting downwards the demand for unskilled workers.

Falk and Koebel estimate a system of input demand functions for five factors of production: materials, capital, unskilled labor (no qualifications), skilled labor (high school degree or equivalent), and high-skilled labor (university degree). Each factor demand is estimated as a function of the prices of all five inputs, the level of output, and a time trend. The main aim of the exercise is to obtain cross-price elasticities of demand, which will tell us whether two inputs are complements or substitutes. The cross-price elasticity is defined as $\epsilon_{ij} = \partial i^* / \partial p_j \cdot p_j / i^*$, where i^* is the amount of factor i demanded and p_j is the price of factor j. A value of $\epsilon_{ij} > 0$ implies that goods i and j are substitutes, while $\epsilon_{ij} < 0$ means that they are complements. The system is estimated for biannual German data, covering the period 1977–1994. The estimated degree of substitutability between material inputs and unskilled labor in the manufacturing and construction sectors is large, with elasticities of substitution respectively equal to 0.14 and 0.34. The demand for high-skilled labor is increased by a lower price of material inputs in manufacturing (with an elasticity of −0.16) and is unaffected in construction. These elasticities imply that a reduction in the price of material inputs would have the effect of shifting upwards the demand for high-skilled workers and downwards that for the unskilled.

German data show, precisely, that since the late 1970s there has been a sharp upwards shift of the demand for high-skilled labor and a downwards shift of the demand for unskilled labor. The period witnessed a rapid decline in the level of employment of unskilled workers, some increase in skilled employment, and a fast rise in high-skilled employment, together with a moderate increase in relative wages (the high-skilled to unskilled wage ratio rose by 6 percent between 1977 and 1994). Can this shift in relative labor demands be explained by a reduction in the price of material inputs? During the sample period, labor costs increased substantially, with the price of unskilled labor increasing by 107 percent and that of highly skilled labor by 123 percent. However, the price of material inputs increased[17] by only 38 percent. The resulting substantial reduction in the price of materials relative to labor costs – it fell by one third, i.e., an average of 2.4 per year, relative to that of unskilled labor – may, therefore, have been a cause of the observed changes in labor demand.

Similar evidence exists for the US. Over the period 1979–1987 the real wage of unskilled workers fell by 6.6 percent (see Katz and

---

[17] The increase in material prices is even smaller, just 13 percent, if we take as a starting point 1980 in order to exclude the 1977–1980 oil price shock.

Murphy, 1992) and real material prices by 16.3 percent (see Revenga, 1992). This means that the price of materials relative to unskilled labor costs decreased by an average of 1.3 percent per year. Unfortunately, there are no tests of the impact of material prices on different labor categories. Revenga (1992) shows that both falling import prices and falling material prices played a significant role in the reduction in the average wage and level of employment in the US manufacturing sector during the period 1980–1987, but a disaggregated analysis is needed in order to understand the relationship between trade and the rise in the skill premium. A more direct test is undertaken by Kramarz (1997). He uses firm-level data to examine whether increased openness is what has caused changes in the relative wages and relative unemployment rates in the French economy. His findings suggest that increases in both the import and export ratios of a firm have a significant, though small, effect on the relative wages paid by the firm and its level of employment.

The extent to which the reduction in the relative price of materials in developed countries is due to trade liberalization has, to our knowledge, not been investigated. Nevertheless, Owens and Wood (1997) provide some insights about the import and export patterns of different countries. They divide traded goods into manufactures and a broad definition of primary products, which includes processed primary products such as gasoline. Primary products represent less than 30 percent of total exports in developed countries and the East-Asian "high-performing" economies. For all other countries, primary commodities account for between 45 percent and 90 percent of all exports. Although the differences are less marked for imports, Owens and Wood show that the share of primary products in total imports tends to increase with the country's income level. The large share of primary products in exports from poorer to richer countries indicates that increased openness and the reduction of trade barriers are an important cause of the decline in the price of material inputs.

Overall, no one has yet produced systematic evidence of an effect of trade on relative labor demands through material prices. Nevertheless, the fact that imports consist of intermediate inputs as well as of final goods implies that the evidence presented by

Berman, Bound, and Griliches (1994) does not suffice to rule out trade liberalization as part of the explanation for the observed rise in wage inequality. Namely, by lowering the cost of purchasing physical input – or by improving the variety (or mix) of physical inputs – trade liberalization may well be partly responsible for the shift in labor demand toward skilled labor even in sectors that do not directly trade with the South but yet are substituting material input for unskilled labor. The shift toward skilled labor is in turn likely to be particularly pronounced if there is complementarity between technological vintages, material inputs, and skills as evidenced by Krusell, Ohanian, Rios-Rull, and Violante (1996) (see section 3.2.2(a) below), in other words if technical progress is both skill biased and also capital embodied.

3.2 Skill-biased technical progress

A competing hypothesis is that the shift in the relative labor demands has been caused by technological change. Now, if technological change is to generate an increase in wage inequality, it must be because technological change is *biased* toward certain skills or specializations, in the sense that it reveals and enhances new differences in abilities among workers across or within educational cohorts.[18]

The empirical literature provides two main pieces of evidence in favor of this hypothesis:

(a) First, the biggest part of the decrease in the proportion of unskilled labor is due to *within-industry* changes, and *not* between-industry shifts (as would be the case if changes in final demand were the most important factor).

(b) Second, the increase in the share of skilled workers within-industry is positively correlated to indicators of technical progress.

The evidence on within-industry changes in relative employment was reviewed in the previous subsection. Although impor-

[18] See Juhn *et al.* (1993) and Piketty (1996).

tant, this is only an indirect test of the role of skill-biased technical progress. More direct evidence is provided by estimates of
equations relating the employment share of non-manual
workers to various indicators of technical change. Berman,
Bound, and Griliches (1994) show that both computer (as a share
of total investment in 1974) and R&D expenditures have a positive and significant impact on the share of non-production
workers:[19] these two factors account for 70 percent of the move
away from production labor over 1979–1987. A similar analysis
for the UK shows that R&D expenditures have a positive and significant impact on the share of non-manuals in employment.[20]
The same results are obtained when technical progress is proxied
by the introduction of microcomputers by firms. This is consistent with Krueger's (1993) findings regarding the return to computer usage. When he includes a computer-use variable into a
human-capital wage equation, he finds that the wage premium
of workers using a computer is highly significant in the US, and
that it increased from 15 percent to 17.6 percent between 1984
and 1989.

Overall, empirical evidence both from the UK and the US indicates that more technologically advanced industries are more
likely to have increased their relative use of skilled workers in the
1980s. We will argue in the next two subsections that this may
come as a result of both disembodied and embodied technical
change.

3.2.1 DISEMBODIED TECHNICAL PROGRESS

The rise in the wage premium for skilled workers raises a theoretical puzzle. Although technological change can exert an
upward pressure on the demand for skilled workers and thereby
increase their wage premium over unskilled workers, education
should eventually lead to an expanded supply of skilled labor
and thereby to a fall in the wage differential.[21] In what follows we

---

[19] All regressions include controls for the level of output and the stock of physical
capital.   [20] See Machin (1995).   [21] See Galor and Tsiddon (1994).

examine how the adoption and implementation of new technologies may result in a situation in which the wage premium grows even when the relative supply of skilled workers is increasing.

3.2.1(a) A basic explanation based on general purpose technologies

In an influential paper on the dynamics of wage inequality in the US labor market, Murphy and Welch (1992) provide evidence that the wage gap between employees with high school degrees only and those who have pursued college studies increased by 25 percent between 1980 and 1990, following a long period during which the same wage gap had stagnated or even decreased.

A natural explanation for this pattern is the acceleration in the diffusion of new "general purpose technologies" (GPTs).[22] Let us pause for a moment and explain in more detail what we have in mind here.

A GPT is a technological invention (or breakthrough) that affects the entire economic system. However, whilst each GPT raises aggregate output and productivity in the long run, it also causes cyclical fluctuations while the economy adjusts to it. Examples of GPTs include the steam engine, the electric dynamo, the laser, and the computer. As argued by economic historians (e.g., David 1990), there are several reasons to believe that the diffusion of a new GPT in to the entire economy, should be *non-linear*. For example, the existence of *strategic complementarities* (or *network externalities*) between the various sectors of the economy may generate temporary lock-in effects, of the kind already emphasized by Shleifer (1986) in his paper on *implementation cycles*. (I do not implement the new GPT as long as no one else does, unless forced to do so by some "exogenous" factor such as the continuous rise in labor costs.)

Another potential source of non-linearity in the diffusion of new GPTs which we formalize below lies in the phenomenon of

---

[22] This analysis draws on Aghion and Howitt (1998), chapter 8.

social learning. That is, the way most firms learn to use a new technology is not to discover everything on their own but to learn from the experience of other firms in a similar situation. For a firm to learn from other firms, the problems to be solved before the technology can successfully be implemented must bear enough resemblance to the problems solved by others so that it is worthwhile trying to use the procedures of those successful firms as a "template" on which to prepare for adoption. Thus, the fact that at first no one knows how to exploit a new GPT means that almost nothing happens in the aggregate. Only minor improvements in knowledge take place for a long time, because successful implementation in any sector requires firms to make independent discoveries with little guidance from the successful experience of others. But if this activity continues for long enough, a point will eventually be reached when almost everyone can see enough other firms using the new technology to make it worth their while experimenting with it. Hence, even though the spread of a new GPT takes place over a long period of time, most of the costly experimentation through which the spread takes place may be concentrated over a relatively short subperiod, during which there is a cascade or *snowball effect* resulting in an *accelerated* demand for skilled labor. This in turn will cause the skill premium to rise.

More formally, suppose that aggregate output is produced by "labor" according to the constant return technology:

$$Y = \left\{ \int_0^1 A(i)^\alpha x(i)^\alpha di \right\}^{\frac{1}{\alpha}}, \qquad (9)$$

where $A(i) = 1$ in sectors where the old GPT is still used, and $A(i) = \gamma > 1$ in sectors that have successfully innovated, while $x(i)$ is manufacturing labor used to produce the intermediate good in sector i. The total labor force L is actually divided into skilled and unskilled workers; whilst old sectors (with $A(i) = 1$) can indifferently use skilled and unskilled workers, the experimentation and the implementation of the new GPT requires skilled labor.

For simplicity, we do not detail the supply side of the labor market, but simply assume that the fraction of skilled workers is monotonically increasing over time, for example as a result of schooling and/or training investments which we do not model here

$$L_s(t) = L(1 - (1 - \tau)e^{-\lambda_2 t}), \quad \tau < 1,$$

where τ is the initial fraction of skilled workers and λ_2 is a positive number measuring the speed of skill acquisition.

We now have to analyze the demand side of the labor market, and in particular determine at any point in time how many sectors are still using the old GPT and therefore do not have any specific need for skilled workers, and how many sectors are experimenting with or already using the new GPT.

We assume that in each sector i, moving from the old to the new GPT requires two steps. First, a firm in that sector must acquire a "template" on which to base experimentation. Second, the firm must use this template to discover how to implement the GPT in that particular sector. Let n_0 denote the fraction of sectors that have not yet acquired a template; n_1 denote the fraction of sectors that have acquired a template but are still experimenting; and $n_2 = 1 - n_0 - n_1$ the fraction of sectors who have succeeded in making the transition to the new GPT.

A sector will acquire a template if a firm in that sector either makes an independent discovery or finds its template by "imitation," that is, by observing at least k "similarly located" firms that have made a successful transition to the new GPT. The Poisson arrival rate of independent discoveries to such a sector is $\lambda_0 < 1$. The Poisson arrival rate of opportunities to observe m similarly located firms is assumed to equal unity. The probability that such an observation will pay off (in other words, the probability that at least k among the m similar firms will have successfully experimented the new GPT) is given by the cumulative binomial

$$\varphi(m,k,n_2) = \sum_{j=k}^{m} \binom{m}{j} n_2^j (1 - n_2)^{m-j},$$

since n_2 is the probability that a randomly selected firm will have succeeded in implementing the new GPT. Thus the flow of sectors that acquire a template and can thus start *experimenting* on the new GPT, will be equal to n_0 times the flow probability of each sector making the transition: $\lambda_0 + \varphi(m,k,n_2)$.

Now we assume that for an experimenting firm to actually succeed in implementing the new GPT, it must employ at least N units of labor per period. We can think of this labor as being used in formal R&D, informal R&D, or in an experimental startup firm. In any case it is not producing current output. Instead, it allows the sector to access a Poisson process that will deliver a workable implementation of the new GPT with an arrival rate of λ_1. Thus the flow of new sectors that can implement the new GPT will be the number of experimenting sectors n_1, times the success rate per sector per unit of time λ_1.

We can summarize the discussion to this point by observing that the evolution over time of the two variables n_1 and n_2 is given by the autonomous system of ordinary differential equations

$$\dot{n}_1 = [\lambda_0 + \varphi(m,k,n_2)](1 - n_1 - n_2) - \lambda_1 n_1$$
$$\dot{n}_2 = \lambda_1 n_1 \tag{N}$$

with initial condition $n_1(0) = 0, n_2(0) = 0$. The time path of n_0 is then given automatically by the identity $n_0 \equiv 1 - n_1 - n_2$.

Figure 6 depicts the solution to the above system (N). Not surprisingly, the time-path of n_2 follows a *logistic* curve, accelerating at first and slowing down as n_2 approaches 1, with the maximal growth rate occurring somewhere in the middle. Likewise the path of n_1 must peak somewhere in the middle of the transition, in as much as it starts and ends at zero. If the arrival rate λ_0 of independent discoveries is very small then both n_1 and n_2 will remain near zero for a long time. Figure 6 displays the behavior of n_1 and n_2 in the case where $\lambda_0 = 0.005, \lambda_1 = 0.3, m = 10$, and $k = 3$. The number of sectors engaging in experimentation peaks sharply in year 20 due to social learning.

The transition process from the old to the new GPT can then be divided into two subperiods. First, in the early phase of transition (i.e., when t is low) the number of sectors using the new GPT is too small to absorb the whole skilled labor force, which in turn implies that a positive fraction of skilled workers will have to be employed by the old sectors at the same wage as their unskilled peers. Thus, during the early phase of transition the labor market

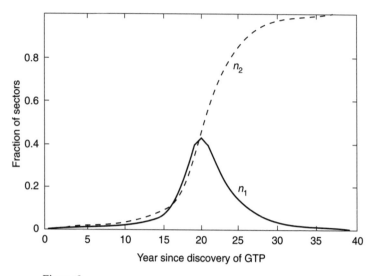

Figure 6

will remain "unsegmented," with the real wage being the *same* for skilled and unskilled labor and determined by the labor-market clearing equation

$$(1 - n_2) \cdot x_0 + n_2 \cdot x_N + n_1 \cdot N = L \tag{L}$$

underbrace: labor demand by an old sector — labor demand by a new sector — labor demand by an experimenting sector

However, in the later phase of transition, where the fraction of new sectors has grown sufficiently large that it can absorb the whole skilled labor force, the labor market will become segmented, with skilled workers being exclusively employed (at a higher wage) by new sectors whilst unskilled workers remain in old sectors. Let w_u and w_s denote the real wages respectively paid to unskilled and skilled workers. We now have

$$w_s > w_u,$$

since the two real wages are determined by two separate labor-market clearing conditions, respectively

$$L_2 = n_1 \cdot N + n_2 x_N \rightarrow w_s$$

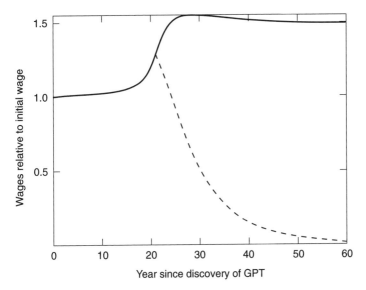

Figure 7
Notes: The solid line indicates the skilled wage, and the dashed line the unskilled wage.

and

$$L_1 = L - L_2 = (1 - n_2) x_0 \rightarrow w_u.$$

Figure 7 depicts the time path of real wages in the benchmark case of the previous subsection with $\lambda_2 = 0.05$ and $\tau = 0.25$.

The skill premium (w_s / w_u) starts increasing sharply in the year $n = 21$ when social learning accelerates the flow of new sectors in the economy, and the premium keeps on increasing although more slowly during the remaining part of the transition process. Since everyone ends up earning the same (skilled) wage, standard measures of wage inequality first rise and then fall.

3.2.1(b) Trade reconsidered

Beyond its direct impact on wage inequality, skill-biased technical change also magnifies the effect of openness to international trade, particularly when the consequences for the supply of skills are

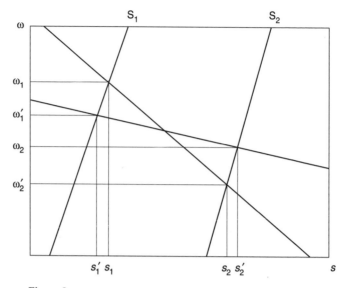

Figure 8

taken into account. Following García-Peñalosa (1996) and Wood and Ridao-Cano (1996), consider a situation in which the relative supply of skilled labor is elastic and increases with the relative wage. This is depicted in figure 8. As the demand for skilled labor in country B (A) increases (decreases), the incentives to accumulate skills change. The effect of opening up to trade would be to increase both the relative wage and the supply of skilled labor in the skill-abundant country, and to reduce the skill premium and the number of skilled workers in the skill-poor economy.

This hypothesis is tested by Wood and Ridao-Cano (1996) for a cross-section of 90 countries over the period 1960–1990. Over this period, enrollment rates increased in all countries. However, trade has affected the dispersion of human capital stocks across countries. Wood and Ridao-Cano find that opening up to trade reduced the proportion of the population in secondary and tertiary education relative to the world average in countries with a small initial stock of skilled labor, while it increased relative enrollment ratios in countries which already had a large educated labor force. These relationships are not only statistically significant but also large in magnitude.

What are the welfare implications of these changes? In a static model, both countries A and B benefit from trade even once the supply responses are taken into account. However, endogenous growth theory tells us that educated labor is precisely what generates technological change. The supply responses would then have the effect of increasing the growth rate in the skill-abundant economy and reducing it in the unskilled labor-rich one.

If technical change is neutral, so that the relative demand for skilled labor is decreasing in the number of skilled workers, as depicted in figure 9, the increase in relative wages caused by increased openness would have a once-and-for-all impact on the supply of skills. As a result, the skill-abundant economy will grow at a constant rate, which is faster than that under autarchy. The skill-poor economy will grow at a slower rate than it did when closed. Trade therefore has two effects on inequality. On the one hand, it increases or decreases inequality within a country, depending on its initial skill endowment relative to that of its trading partner. On the other hand, it always increases cross-country inequality as it raises the growth rate of the richer economy and reduces that of the poor one.

The initial impact of increased openness on relative wages is likely to be small, as the evidence shows, but its effects are magnified if technical change is skill biased. In this case, the relative demand for skilled labor shifts outwards as the level of technology increases (see subsection 3.2.1a). This means that opening up to trade will affect the *rate of change* of relative wages and of the supply of skills. Consider the skill-abundant economy. Trade increases the demand for skilled labor and hence the relative skilled wage. This has the effect of increasing the supply of skilled workers and the rate of growth of the technology. But since technical change shifts the demand for educated labor, the wage ratio will increase further, resulting in an even higher stock of skilled labor and a faster rate of growth, and so on. Skill-biased *disembodied* technical change thus reinforces the impact of free trade on wages, skilled labor supplies, and growth, resulting in an *increasing* skill premium, educated labor force, and growth rate.

As we argued at the end of subsection 3.1, trade- and skill-biased *embodied* technical change may also be mutually reinforcing in pushing up the skill premium, especially when physical inputs (either directly imported from the south or whose production benefits from cheaper access to material inputs from the south) involved in the implementation of new technologies are both *substitutable for unskilled labor* and *complementary to skilled labor*. This brings us to the next subsection on skill-biased *embodied* technical progress and to the pioneering work by Krusell *et al.* (1996).

3.2.2 EMBODIED TECHNICAL PROGRESS

3.2.2(a) Skill-biased technical change and the aggregate production function

A standard assumption in both the traditional and the more recent growth literature is that technological change is "neutral." New technologies therefore shift the aggregate production function, increasing the productivity of all factors to the same extent. However, the model presented in subsection 3.2.1(a) has taught us that firms that introduce new technologies may require a different type of workers than those firms which continue to implement old technologies. The question then is how we can capture this difference in the degree of complementarity within an aggregate production function, and what it implies for the observed parameter values.

Krusell *et al.* (1996) propose a very attractive formulation. Consider an economy in which output is given by

$$Y_t = A_t f(q_t k_t, u_t, s_t). \tag{10}$$

where k_t denotes the capital input, u_t is unskilled labor, and s_t is skilled labor. There is a common technology factor that affects the productivity of all production factors equally, A_t, and a capital-specific one, q_t. The latter represents *embodied technical change*, i.e., innovations that require new machinery to implement them. It can, for example, be understood as a measure of the *quality* of the capital input which is subject to improvement over time. If the degree of complementarity between equipment and skilled labor were different from that between equipment and unskilled workers, then embodied technical change would affect the demand for the two types of labor differently. That is, technical change would be biased.

Assume that the production function is given by a "nested CES" technology, which allows for a different degree of complementarity between the two types of labor and equipment,

$$f(q_t k_t, u_t, s_t) = [\mu u_t^\sigma + (1 - \mu)(\lambda(q_t k_t)^\rho + (1 - \lambda)s_t^\rho)^{\sigma/\rho}]^{1/\sigma}, \quad (11)$$

where $\sigma < 1$ and $\rho < 1$.

If $\sigma = \rho = 0$, then $f(.)$ would simply be a Cobb–Douglas function of the three inputs. However, if the parameters are above zero, there is greater substitutability than under Cobb–Douglas. For $\sigma > \rho$, equipment capital is more complementary with skilled labor than with unskilled workers. The opposite holds if $\sigma < \rho$.

We are interested in how technical change affects the skill premium, that is, the ratio of skilled to unskilled wages. Define the skill premium as $\omega_t \equiv w_t^s / w_t^u$. Then

$$\omega_t = \frac{\partial f(.)/\partial s_t}{\partial f(.)/\partial u_t} = \frac{(1 - \mu)(1 - \lambda)}{\mu}\left(\lambda\left(\frac{q_t k_t}{s_t}\right)^\rho + (1 - \lambda)\right)^{\sigma/\rho - 1}\left(\frac{u_t}{s_t}\right)^{1 - \sigma}. \quad (12)$$

To find the impact of a change in the amount of equipment used or its quality, differentiate equation (12) to get

$$\frac{\partial \omega_t}{\partial k_t} = (\sigma - \rho)\frac{\omega_t}{k_t}\left(1 + \frac{1 - \lambda}{\lambda}\left(\frac{s_t}{q_t k_t}\right)^\rho\right)^{-1}, \quad (13)$$

$$\frac{\partial \omega_t}{\partial q_t} = (\sigma - \rho)\frac{\omega_t}{q_t}\left(1 + \frac{1 - \lambda}{\lambda}\left(\frac{s_t}{q_t k_t}\right)^\rho\right)^{-1}. \quad (14)$$

It is clear from equations (13) and (14) that the effect of an increase in equipment or its quality on the skill premium depends on the complementarity of the latter with the two types of labor. If it is more complementary with skilled labor, that is $\sigma > \rho$, then the above derivatives are positive, implying that more/better equipment increases the wage of skilled workers by more than it increases the wage of unskilled workers. If $\sigma < \rho$, then more/better equipment reduces ω_t.

Krusell *et al.* (1996) estimate the production function given by equation (11) using US data for the period 1964–1992. They find that unskilled labor is more substitutable with capital than skilled labor, that is, $\sigma > \rho$. The estimate of ρ is negative, indicating that human capital and physical capital are complements, while the estimate of σ is positive, implying that unskilled labor and machinery are substitutes.

Moreover, taking logarithms of equation (12), the growth rate of the skill premium can be written as

$$g_{\omega t} \simeq (1 - \sigma)(g_{ut} - g_{st}) + \lambda(\sigma - \rho)(g_{kt} + g_{qt} - g_{st}). \tag{15}$$

The rate of growth of the skill premium depends on the relative growth rates of the supplies of the both of labor, g_{ut} and g_{st} (standard effect). Since $1 > \sigma$, faster (relative) growth of skilled labor reduces the skill premium. There is also a term capturing the capital–skill complementarity. Since $\sigma > \rho$, faster growth of q_t, for a given rate of growth of the stock of skilled labor, raises the skill premium. Hence, embodied technical change is skill biased.

The implications of embodied technical change can be far reaching. We have just seen how it can explain the dynamics of wage inequality *across* different education cohorts (i.e., between skilled and unskilled workers). It can also be used to understand the evolution of wage inequality *within* educational cohorts.

3.2.2(b) Embodied technical change and within-group inequality

Skill-biased technological change as analyzed in subsection 3.2.1, cannot account for the fact that around 60 percent of the total increase in wage inequality over the past twenty years is *within* groups of individuals with apparently the same education level and the same number of working years (Juhn, Murphy, and Pierce (1993)).[23]

Now, one might go on and argue that this empirical observation reflects measurement problems. In particular the existing studies do not properly discriminate between schools and universities

---

[23] The next three subsections draw from Aghion and Howitt (1998), chapters 9 and 10.

with different levels of standing. As pertinent as such a criticism may be, it cannot entirely account, however, for the magnitude of the within-cohort effects; nor does it account for the fact that the wage gap between workers initially hired by the same firm at the same wage, is also increasing over time.

In a very interesting paper, Violante (1996) develops a new explanation for the increasing wage dispersion *within* educational groups during the past twenty-five years in the United States. This explanation is based on the notion of vintage-specific skills primarily acquired by workers through learning-by-doing. More specifically, suppose that technological knowledge is embodied in equipments of different vintages. Workers are *ex-ante* identical (they share the same educational background), but then are randomly matched with machines of different vintages and become increasingly heterogenous as their specific labor-market histories unfold, involving different patterns of accumulation or transfer of skills on the job and between jobs. Indeed, workers can either remain on the same job and improve their skills on the current machine through learning-by-doing or move to newer machines. New machines are more productive than old machines, but leaving an old machine involves a (partial) loss of skills for the worker.

By means of calibrations, Violante finds that the higher the rate of technological change, the higher the (steady-state) variance of wages. The basic intuition for this finding can be summarized as follows. As technological progress speeds up, the cross-sectional variance of productivity across vintages increases. This implies, first, that high-skilled workers are more likely to turn down old vintages and instead keep searching for jobs in newer vintages (or "lines"), and, second, that due to decreasing returns to learning-by-doing on any particular vintage, the high-skilled workers (who work on newer vintages than low-skilled workers) will improve their productivity faster than the low-skilled. At the same time, being increasingly remote from the leading edge, less-skilled workers will be less able to transfer their previous skills to newer vintages, and therefore will be less willing to move from old to new vintages. This, in turn, will generate an increased variance in productivity, and thus in wages, among workers with different matching and vintage histories.

3.2.2(c) A simple model of earnings inequality based on vintage effects

The following formalization might help develop more precise intuitions on the effects of technical change and education policy on *within*-cohorts wage inequality.[24]

The most basic model of technical change with vintage effects we have in mind can be described as follows. There is a single final good, which can be used only for consumption, and a continuum of intermediate goods (or "machines") of different vintages, which constitute the only inputs to producing the final good. More recent vintages are better (i.e., more productive) than old ones because they embody a higher level of general knowledge. The arrival rate of new vintages (i.e., of new fundamental discoveries) is exogenous, equal to $g > 0$, and we are focusing on a steady-state path in which general knowledge is also growing at rate g.

Let $A_\tau = e^{g\tau}$ denote the leading-edge technology producing at date τ; let Z_a denote the "quality" of a worker on a line of age a: that is, labor input ℓ_a on a line of age a produces $Z_a(\ell_a)^\alpha$ units of intermediate good of the corresponding vintage.[25] Thus aggregate final output at date t is simply

$$Y_t = \int_{-\infty}^{t} A_\tau \cdot Z_{t-\tau}(\ell_{t-\tau})^\alpha d\tau = \int_{-\infty}^{t} Y_{t,\tau} d\tau,$$

where the parameter α lies between 0 and 1.

The quality of workers on a newly invented vintage is $q_0 > 0$, and quality improvements are vintage specific and come at a rate equal to the amount of learning-by-doing in the economy, which we normalize to one: $dZ_a / da = 1$. Thus, the quality of workers on a line of age a is

$$Z_a = q_0 + a.$$

The wage of someone working on a product line of vintage τ when that vintage is a years old is the marginal value product

---

[24] This section is somewhat more technical than the others and therefore might be skipped in a first reading.

[25] The initial allocation of workers to lines is assumed to be purely random.

$$w(a,\tau) = e^{gt}\alpha(q_0 + a)\ell_a^{\alpha-1},$$

where the number of workers on the product line is $\ell_a = \ell_0 e^{-\sigma a}$, and σ is the maximum rate at which workers can relocate to the leading edge. *Thus, not all workers can move to the leading edge and this is the primary source of within-cohort inequality.* We call those workers for whom it is possible to relocate to another vintage "upgraded workers."

The expected value of future wages until the next move, that is, until the worker has the opportunity of moving to the leading edge, to a worker now on the leading edge at date t is

$$v_1 = e^{gt} \cdot \int_0^\infty e^{-(\rho+\sigma)a}(\alpha(q_0 + a)(\ell_0 \cdot e^{-\sigma a})^{\alpha-1})\,da,$$

where ρ denotes the individual rate of time preference.

The expected value of future wages until the next move to a worker now on a product line of age Δ at date t is

$$v_1(\Delta) = e^{g(t-\Delta)} \cdot \int_\Delta^\infty e^{-(\rho+\sigma)(a-\Delta)}(\alpha(q_0 + a)(\ell_0 \cdot e^{-\sigma a})^{\alpha-1})\,da.$$

The ratio of these two expected present values is the relative value of staying on the old technology

$$v(\Delta) = \frac{v_1(\Delta)}{v_1} = \frac{(q_0 + \Delta)(\rho + \sigma\alpha) + 1}{q_0(\rho + \sigma\alpha) + 1}e^{-\Delta(g-\sigma(1-\alpha))}.$$

Using this formula, we can divide the parameter space into three regions, corresponding to three different cases.

Case 1

$$g > \sigma(1-\alpha) + \frac{\rho + \sigma\alpha}{q_0(\rho + \sigma\alpha) + 1}.$$

In that case the relocation constraint is binding, in other words all those workers that have the opportunity to relocate to the leading-edge will do so. This, in turn, implies that $v(\Delta)$ is monotonically decreasing with Δ, which means that lifetime earnings will also decrease monotonically with age. Furthermore, *the higher the growth rate, the more unequal the lifetime earnings of workers across different lines:* indeed the ratio $v(\Delta)$ decreases faster with Δ as g increases. Violante's conjecture is thus automatically validated in that case.

However, the relationship between growth and (lifetime earnings) inequality becomes somewhat more involved when

$$g < \sigma(1-\alpha) + \frac{\rho + \sigma\alpha}{q_0(\rho + \sigma\alpha) + 1}.$$

Case 2

$$g < \sigma(1-\alpha).$$

In this case the relative value $v(\Delta)$ of staying on a line of age Δ, conditional on *all* upgraded workers systematically relocating to newer vintages, would become monotonically *increasing* in Δ, which in turn is a contradiction: indeed, why would upgraded workers decide to move to newer vintages if doing so leads to a lower expected value of future wages? (We implicitly assume that upgraded workers always have the right *not* to relocate to newer vintages.) As it turns out, the relocation constraint is no longer binding, and the equilibrium will involve having only a *fraction* of upgraded workers relocate to newer lines, in such a way that workers will end up being indifferent between relocating to *any* line: this in turn will result in *complete equality of lifetime earnings across different lines.*

To see this in slightly greater detail, let us reason by contradiction and suppose that there is some line X to which nobody wishes to relocate (because the lifetime wage on that line is lower than on other lines). Then, the fact that some workers are constantly relocating to the newest lines (this must be true because the marginal productivity of labor on new lines goes to infinity when $\ell_0 \to 0$) means that the relative value of staying on line X is constantly increasing relative to the value of relocating to the newest lines (because $g < \sigma^*(1-\alpha)$ – where $\sigma^*(<\sigma)$ is the actual relocation rate in equilibrium – and therefore $v(\Delta)$ increases with Δ). This in turn implies that it cannot be an equilibrium for all workers to avoid line X.

Therefore, when $g < \sigma(1-\alpha)$ an increase in the rate of growth g

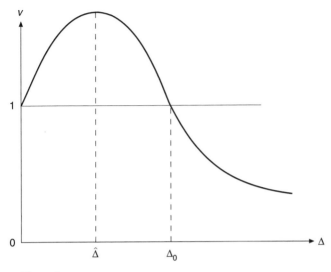

Figure 9

will have no effect on earnings inequality because inequality stays equal to zero in that case.

Case 3

$$\sigma(1-\alpha) < g < \sigma(1-\alpha) + \frac{\rho + \sigma\alpha}{q_0(\rho + \sigma\alpha) + 1}.$$

In this case, the relative value $v(\Delta)$ of staying on a line of age Δ, conditional on *all* upgraded workers relocating to newer vintages, becomes non-monotonic, as shown in figure 9, where $\hat{\Delta}$ is the product line age that maximizes $v(\Delta)$.[26]

This again implies that it cannot be an equilibrium for *all* upgraded workers and in particular for those currently working on lines of age $\Delta < \hat{\Delta}$ to systematically relocate to the leading edge. Instead, *one can show the existence* of a non-empty interval of recent vintages $[0,\bar{\Delta}]$ to which workers relocate (randomly), but no one will voluntarily relocate to an older vintage. The expected present value of earnings on a line of age Δ in equilibrium, EPV(Δ), will then vary with age according to figure 10.

---

[26] That is, $\hat{\Delta}$ satisfies $g = \sigma(1-\alpha) + (\rho + \sigma\alpha)/((q_0 + \hat{\Delta})(\rho + \sigma\alpha) + 1)$.

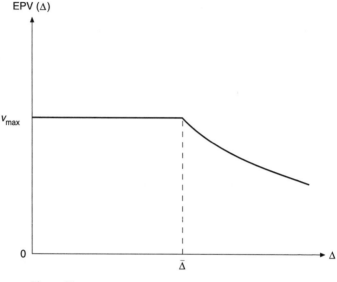

Figure 10

Indeed, all sufficiently new lines will continue to attract new relocating workers until the expected present value of earnings for workers on those lines has been bid down to equality with newer lines. However, beyond some $\bar{\Delta} \geq \hat{\Delta}$ nobody will voluntarily relocate to a line of age $\Delta > \bar{\Delta}$ because doing so would depress the relative value of staying on that line even further below the value $v(\Delta)$ indicated in figure 9.

Now an increase in the rate of growth g will shift the curve $EPV(\Delta)/v_{max}$ to the left (as shown in figure 11). So fewer lines will share in the high earnings v_{max}; furthermore, the expected present value of earnings $EPV(\Delta)$ will decrease more rapidly with age Δ for $\Delta > \hat{\Delta}$. Overall, *an increased growth rate will have the unambiguous effect of increasing earnings inequality.*

Remark

Throughout this subsection we have assumed that new knowledge is entirely appropriated by firms (or vintages). In current work with G. L. Violante and Peter Howitt, we can show that in the case where new knowledge is entirely appropriated by workers and transferred by them upon moving from old to new

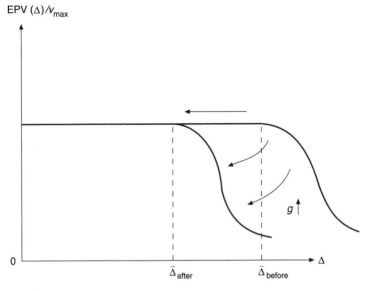

Figure 11

vintages, then the relationship between productivity growth (g) and wage inequality (e.g., measured by the log of the variance of wages across workers) becomes U-shaped as shown in figure 12.

More specifically, what happens is that for low levels of g the reallocation constraint imposed by σ is not binding. Then, a small increase in g will stimulate workers' reallocation to new vintages which in turn *reduces* wage inequality, both because we get closer to perfect equality at the leading-edge wage and because of decreasing returns to labor on each line, including new lines.[27] The reason why this negative effect of g on wage inequality did not operate in the previous case, is simply that when firms appropriate all the knowledge and therefore wages are vintage specific and not worker specific, then there is already perfect wage equality across workers whenever the reallocation constraint ($\sigma^* \leq \sigma$) is not binding!

[27] See appendix 3 for a formal proof in the context of a toy discrete-time-version of the model in this subsection.

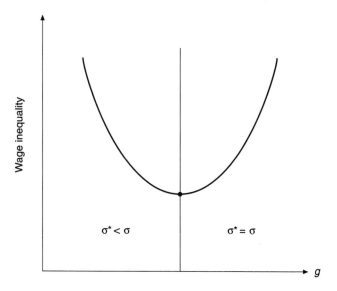

Figure 12

3.2.2(d) Vintage effects and the relationship between education and earnings inequality

The basic model of skill-biased technical progress outlined in subsection 3.2.1(a) implied that education will have the unambiguous effect of reducing wage inequality between skilled and unskilled workers. However, the relationship between education and inequality becomes more subtle and, we believe, also more interesting in the case where technical progress is embodied in particular product lines or vintages and the mobility of developers between those lines is limited.

In the previous subsection, we argued that an exogenous increase in the rate of growth g should result in a higher degree of earnings inequality across (skilled) workers on different product lines. What about the effects of increasing education spending?

The answer to this question will depend on the particular kind (or design) of public support for education. To begin with, any education or training policy that increases the growth rate g without changing the cut-off values $\sigma (1 - \alpha)$ and

$\sigma(1 - \alpha) + \frac{\rho + \sigma\alpha}{q_0(\rho + \sigma\alpha) + 1}$ derived in subsection 3.2.2(c), will automatically *increase* earnings inequality.

More interesting are the effects of education policies aimed at increasing the adaptability of workers to new lines, in other words which result into increasing the value of the mobility parameter σ. There does not seem to be any major loss of economic insight in restricting the analysis to the case where

$$g > \sigma(1 - \alpha) + \frac{\rho + \sigma\alpha}{q_0(\rho + \sigma\alpha) + 1} = E(\sigma),$$

so that in equilibrium the ratio between the expected present values of earnings (until the next upgrading opportunity) for a worker currently on a product line of age Δ and for a worker currently at the leading edge, is given by

$$v(\Delta) = \frac{(q_0 + \Delta)(\rho + \sigma\alpha) + 1}{q_0(\rho + \sigma\alpha) + 1} \cdot e^{-\Delta(g - \sigma(1 - \alpha))},$$

which decreases with Δ when $g > E(\sigma)$, as depicted in figure 13.

We see that, for given g, $v(\Delta)$ decreases less rapidly with Δ the higher σ,[28] in other words, increasing worker mobility *reduces* earnings inequality. Intuitively, as mobility increases and therefore more workers leave their current line to relocate at the leading edge, the productivity of non-upgraded workers on old lines increases more rapidly (remember that the production of any intermediate good involves decreasing returns with respect to labor, i.e., $\alpha < 1$); this in turn will have a boosting effect on future wages of the non-upgraded workers compared to those of workers at the leading edge. Let us thus refer to this effect as a *decreasing return effect*.

Whether the *decreasing return effect* or the *growth effect* dominates will obviously depend on the parameters of the model. In particular, the growth effect will dominate when λ^r or H are sufficiently large and the decreasing return effect will dominate when λ^r and H are small and α is bounded away from zero.

To summarize our analysis in this subsection: (a) educational policy will not systematically be growth enhancing, although it

---

[28] Indeed, $v(\Delta)$ is the product of two terms, the first of which increases more rapidly with Δ the higher σ, and the second (the exponential term) of which decreases less rapidly with Δ as σ increases.

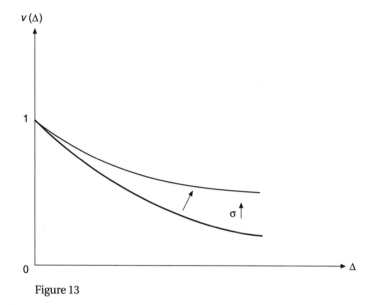

Figure 13

can always be made so through adequate design and targeting;
(b) educational policy – even when aimed at increasing adaptability and mobility of workers across lines – may sometimes
result in a higher degree of inequality across workers employed
on different vintages. Yet, although more elitist (e.g., research-ori-
ented) education policies will unambiguously increase inequality, the overall impact of mobility-enhancing policies will be more
ambiguous as it results from two counteracting effects, namely a
decreasing returns effect whereby mobility reduces earnings
inequality and a growth effect whereby mobility enhances
inequality.

So, both disembodied and embodied technical change are
likely to have contributed to the rise in wage inequality experienced by many OECD countries from the 1980s.

3.3 Labor-market institutions

The empirical literature has put forward one more explanation
for rising wage inequality: the role of changes in labor-market

institutions. It relies on the observation that demand-based explanations (i.e., explanations stressing the increase in skill demand due to trade liberalization or skill-biased technical/organizational change) cannot easily account for some empirical puzzles, such as the differences between the US and UK versus France and Germany pointed out in the previous subsection. Since most industrialized countries were presumably exposed to similar shocks over the period, the American and British experiences require further explanation.

We have seen that the flexibility strategy chosen by firms stands as an interesting explanatory avenue. Another one (surprisingly forgotten in the theoretical literature) focuses on the specific sets of institutions within which countries operate. Since these can mitigate the impact of supply and demand changes on the structure of wages, institutional changes may become sources of rising wage inequality. The 1980s have indeed seen dramatic changes in labor-market institutions both in the United States and in the United Kingdom. They can be summarized as follows:

> The unionization rate fell from 25 to 16 percent in the US between 1979 and 1985, whereas it had lost only 4 percentage points over the previous nineteen years and remained roughly constant in the 1990s.[29] The proportion of trade union members in the UK, though much higher in absolute terms, also fell sharply in the 1980s: from 54 percent in 1980 to 32 percent in 1995.[30] In 1980, 61 percent of British manual employees worked in workplaces where a trade union was recognized for collective bargaining purposes. By 1990, it had fallen to 48 percent (equivalent figures for non-manuals are 50 percent in 1980 and 43 percent in 1990).
>
> In parallel, the importance of the minimum wage legislation has been severely downgraded in both countries in the 1980s. In the US, the real value of the minimum wage decreased by 30 percent during the 1980s. While its relative value had hovered between 42 and 54 percent of average hourly wages in manufacturing throughout the

---

[29] See DiNardo, Fortin, and Lemieux (1996).   [30] See Machin (1997a).

1960s and 1970s,[31] it fell precipitously from 43 percent in 1981 down to 31 percent in 1990. A similar pattern arises from British data. The ratio of minimum pay rates (set up by the so-called Wage Councils) to economy-wide average wages fell from 0.48 in 1979 to 0.40 in 1992 before the system was abolished in 1993.

Several pieces of work have tried to assess the role of declining labor-market institutions in the unprecedented rise in wage inequality experienced by Anglo-Saxon economies. Though it has long been noted that establishments in which unions bargain with the management tend to have more compressed wage structures than non-union establishments, the impact of unionization on wage inequality is a widely debated issue. Indeed, unionization has two opposite effects on wage dispersion. Since the variance of wages is lower in the union sector than in the non-union one, a higher proportion of unionized workers tends to reduce the overall variance in wages. However, a bigger proportion of union members raises the dispersion between union and non-union workers which pushes up the overall variance in wages. Which effect dominates depends on the relative wage level of union workers and on the size of the unionized/non-unionized labor forces.

Fortin and Lemieux (1997) show that the inequality-reducing effect dominates the inequality-enhancing one. They compute the effect of deunionization on the variance of wages by replacing the 1988 unionization rate by its higher 1979 level. Their results show that the variance of log wages would have increased by 21.3 percent less if the rate of unionization had remained at its 1979 level. This result is in line with previous findings of DiNardo, Fortin, and Lemieux (1996) with a more sophisticated methodology, which display an effect ranging from 14 to 21 percent of the variance in wages. Card (1992) and Freeman (1993) also find that deunionization accounts for about one fifth of the increase in wage inequality over the 1980s. Evidence from the UK proves very similar. Gosling and Machin (1995) find that about 20 percent of the rise in wage inequality can be attributed to union decline and

---

[31] See Fortin and Lemieux (1997).

Machin (1997a) stresses that the rise would have been two fifths less over 1983–1991 had the level of union recognition remained at its 1983 level.

Unionization has two indirect effects on wage dispersion through its impact on training and technology adoption, on the one hand, and on the minimum wage, on the other.[32] In the context of a vintage model, training can play the same role as the education policies examined in subsection 3.2.2(d). If unions can exert pressure on employers to provide training that increases the adaptability of workers to new lines, mobility is enhanced and earnings inequality is reduced for any given rate of technical change. Moreover, pressure to provide training would force employers to rely on internal rather than external labor markets in response to shocks and would, as argued in the previous subsection, reduce wage dispersion. There is, to our knowledge, no evidence on the impact of the amount of training on wage inequality.

Unions also have the effect of increasing minimum wages, hence it is not surprising that those countries where union membership has declined have also witnessed a reduction in the real value of minimum wages. The minimum wage sets an explicit floor to the wage distribution, and, by acting as a backstop for its bottom end, it tends to reduce wage dispersion. The magnitude of the impact of a change in the minimum wage depends on its level relative to other wages and on the number of workers affected. Using the same method as for unionization, Fortin and Lemieux (1997) assess the impact of the sharp decrease in the minimum wage experienced by the US, simulating what the distribution of wages would have been in 1988 if its higher 1979 level had prevailed. They find that, if the real value of the minimum wage in 1979 had prevailed in 1988, the variance of wages would have increased by 39.3 percent less than it actually did. This effect is slightly larger than the one found by Card and Krueger (1995) who conclude that 20–30 percent of the rise in wage dispersion can be attributed to the decline in the real value of the minimum wage. It is however in line with the results obtained by Mishel, Bernstein,

[32] See Machin (1997b).

and Schmitt (1996). For a panel of British Wage Council industries in the 1970s and 1980s, Machin and Manning (1994) regress the log of the wage dispersion on a measure of the toughness of the minimum wage system.[33] They find a significantly negative impact of the latter. Depending on the specification, it accounts for 9–20 percent of the rise in dispersion across sectors over the sample period.

These results strongly suggest that at least part of the 1980s rise in wage inequality can be attributed to the weakening of labor-market institutions. The exact mechanism through which this has happened is, as yet, not clear. In particular, the fact that deunion-ization has not resulted in a change in the income shares of labor and capital, but rather altered the shares of different types of workers, makes us question traditional explanations. A plausible hypothesis is that labor-market institutions can magnify or reduce the impact of changes in demand, such as those caused by skill-biased technical change. In particular, when wage disper-sion within cohorts is caused by differences in the vintage of the equipment used by different producers in a sector, centralized bargaining in the sector, by compressing wages, will reduce the impact that a faster rate of growth of knowledge would have on dispersion.

One question remains open: are changes in labor-market insti-tutions exogenous or do they respond to economic factors? Deunionization appears to be a consequence of a change in labor-market conditions and presumably it has been fostered both by the rise in unemployment during the mid 1970s and by the increased segmentation of the labor market since that period. Both phenomena can be seen as by-products of a non-linear process of skill-biased technological diffusion of the kind described in subsection 3.2 above.[34] Nevertheless, the marked differences in the responses of countries such as France and Germany versus the UK and the US, both in terms of the evolution

[33] The toughness of the minimum wage system is measured by the log of the ratio of the minimum wage to average wages. All regressions include a time trend and a measure of aggregate GDP growth.

[34] See Aghion and Howitt (1998), chapter 8, where we argue that the (risky) experi-mentation of new GPT may lead to an accelerated increase in aggregate unem-ployment during the "snowball" phase of the cycle.

of their institutions and the degree to which wages and unemployment have been affected, suggest that underlying social and political attitudes play a major role in shaping labor-market behavior.

3.4 Organizational change

The preceding analysis of skill-biased technical progress and wage inequality may appear too simplistic in its representation of firms as "production functions" in which educational skills *and* current wages are both being taken as given. The reality is indeed more complex as: (i) skills are only partly acquired through education, and are to a substantial extent firm specific, that is, specific to the particular type of production activity and also to the *organizational* form chosen by enterprises; (ii) accordingly, wages are not entirely market determined, but instead result from complex bargaining processes that are also affected by the organizational structure of firms.[35]

In recent years, a growing literature has emphasized the impact of organizational change upon rising wage inequality.[36] The underlying idea is that, as changes in organization take place, the productivity gap increases between individuals with different skill levels. In this subsection we would like to discuss briefly the impact of *organizational change* on wage inequality. In what follows we will put forward two hypotheses:

> In recent years, organizational change has been made possible by the development of new technologies. Hence, it does not stand as an autonomous event but rather as a reaction to other shocks. In particular, it can be understood as being itself the result of skill-biased technical change.
> Whether organizational considerations magnify or dampen the effect of skill-biased technical change on wage

[35] See Stole and Zwiebel (1996).
[36] See for example Kremer and Maskin (1996), Acemoglu (1996), or Lindbeck and Snower (1996).

inequality depends on the relative importance of across-firm effects compared to within-firm effects, and on whether employment flexibility is higher within or between firms.

3.4.1 SOME STYLIZED FACTS ABOUT ORGANIZATIONAL CHANGE

Recent development in the structure of US companies has been characterized by the following trends:

(a) A move toward flatter organizations with both decentralization of decision making within firms (creation of independent profit centers with greater flexibility, and authority being allocated to units' managers) and a decrease in the number of hierarchical layers accompanied by a wider *span of control* at each layer. (By *span of control* we mean the number of downstream agents or units that are being supervised or monitored by a given layer.)[37]

(b) A shift away from hierarchical into more "organic" structures characterized by the replacement of vertical communication channels by *horizontal* (cross-department) *channels*, less hierarchy, and a reduction in specialization (i.e., of the extent to which a particular agent can be identified with any particular task).[38]

(c) A growing segregation of workers by skills, leading to a higher homogeneity of firms' skill/employment structure. Economic activity has shifted away from firms like General Motors which use both high- and low-skilled workers to firms such as Microsoft and McDonald's whose workforces are much more homogenous. In the US, the correlation between wages of production workers in the *same* manufacturing plant rose from 0.76 in 1975 to 0.80 in 1986.[39]

---

[37] See Scott, O'Shaughnessy, and Cappelli (1996).   [38] See Piore (1988).
[39] See Kremer and Maskin (1996).

These trends can be seen as a consequence of technological change.[40] For example, the flattening of firms' structure may result from a higher efficiency in *monitoring* which allows any given principal to increase his span of control and hence to reduce the number of intermediate supervisory layers.[41] The move toward less hierarchical (more organic) firms is also linked to the development of new technologies, insofar as these reduce *communication* costs. A major comparative advantage of a non-hierarchical structure (think, for example, of an assembly line) over a hierarchical one lies in the former's ability to process new information more quickly and thereby to respond faster to changes in demand. This comparative advantage is enhanced when communication costs are reduced, as illustrated by Bolton and Dewatripont (1994). Finally, as technical change takes place, skill homogeneity tends to increase within firms. Kremer and Maskin (1996) show that, in such circumstances, segregated equilibria will emerge, characterized by "assortative matching." Three ingredients are necessary for this to happen: the production process requires two tasks which are complementary, these tasks are unequally sensitive to skills, and the various skill levels are imperfect substitutes. Under such conditions, when skill dispersion reaches a certain threshold, cross matching of workers with

[40] Another cause of organizational change are human-capital advances. First, a greater availability of well-educated workers who can process information about new projects at a lower cost makes it profitable for firm owners and/or top managers to delegate some decision rights to lower layers of the hierarchy, hence flattening the firm's structure (see Aghion and Tirole 1997). Second, human-capital advances increase the relative advantage of organic structures, characterized by task diversification and more autonomy awarded to workers. The scope of the range of tasks performed by workers depends on the tradeoff between returns to specialization and returns to diversification (Lindbeck and Snower, 1996). Suppose that productivity is an increasing function of exposure to a task (specialization) and of the variety of tasks performed (diversification). If human-capital advances make workers more flexible, the returns to diversification will increase and organic firms are bound to develop at the expense of "taylorist" (hierarchical) ones. More generally, if the reduced division of labor goes along with more autonomy being awarded to workers, the supply of skilled (educated) workers in the economy becomes a crucial determinant of firms' organizational choice (Caroli *et al.*, 1997).

[41] Greater efficiency in monitoring may be due to new monitoring technologies which make it possible for a principal to directly monitor more agents, or to an increase in total factor productivity, which increases workers' incentive to exert effort and thus requires a lower degree of monitoring (Acemoglu and Newman, 1997).

different skill levels is replaced by assortative matching: high- and low-skilled workers are employed by different firms in which the labor force is perfectly homogenous.

Technical progress can then be seen as having two effects on wage inequality: a direct one, examined in subsection 3.2, and an indirect one through induced changes in firms' organizational structures that may amplify or dampen the direct effect. Given that technical progress tends to be skill biased, one could conjecture that organizational change will necessarily increase wage inequality. We will challenge this view in the next subsection, arguing that the consequences of organizational change heavily depend on the choice made by firms regarding human resources flexibility.

3.4.2 ORGANIZATIONAL CHANGE AND WAGE INEQUALITY: THE ROLE OF INTERNAL VERSUS EXTERNAL FLEXIBILITY

One argument in favor of the view that organizational change necessarily fosters wage inequality is that non-hierarchical firms rely on direct, horizontal communication among workers and on task diversification as opposed to specialization. They hence require highly *polyvalent* agents, who can both perform varied tasks *and* learn from other agents' activities. If educated workers have a relative advantage at polyvalence, they will get a premium in such organizations.[42] This is likely to be the case since education is, by far, the main provider of the kind of general knowledge that is required for a worker to be truly polyvalent.

A second reason why organizational change may be at the root of rising inequality has to do with skill segregation. As the within-firm skill structure tends to become more homogenous, the productivity gap across firms increases. Assume that the economy is initially in a situation where all types of workers are employed together and that it then moves toward segregated firms. Segregation takes place between high-skill (and sometimes high-

[42] See Scott *et al.* (1996).

physical capital[43]) enterprises and mixed or low-skill firms. Since the former are more productive than the latter, all other things being equal, wage inequality is bound to increase across firms within an industry.[44] This suggests that organizational change may itself be *skill biased* and draws, in turn, a causal relationship between the spreading of more organic (and highly homogenous) firms *and* the rise in wage inequality.

However, strong arguments point in favor of a reverse relationship. If task diversification implies that highly skilled workers are employed in activities in which their relative advantage is lower, it might lead to a reduction in educational wage inequality.[45] More importantly, as decision rights are delegated to lower layers of the hierarchy, firm owners need to avoid moral hazard (or free-riding problems) in teams. The outcome in terms of wage inequality will heavily depend on the choice of the delegees. The owner may choose to concentrate the delegated rights on a small number of "team leaders." This unevenness in authority allocation will, in turn, result in an increased wage differential between the team leader and his co-team members,[46] all of whom are likely to be drawn from the same educational cohort.[47] On the contrary, it may be optimal to delegate those rights to a large number of team members. In this case, incentive considerations may lead to a rise in wages for workers in the lower part of the occupational structure and, hence, to a narrowing of the corresponding wage gap. This prediction is actually in accordance with the results displayed by Cappelli and Daniel (1995) on US data. They show that the ratio of supervisors to blue-collar workers' wages is significantly lower in those firms which have introduced Total Quality Management schemes.[48]

When supervisory layers are removed, whether the wage differential between top managers (or top supervisors) and the downstream teams should increase or decrease will also depend

---

[43] See Acemoglu (1996).   [44] See Caroli (1997).   [45] See Caroli *et al.* (1997).
[46] This is most likely to be the case whenever: (a) employees are highly responsive to monetary incentives and do not only value the private benefits of control (see Aghion and Tirole (1997)); (b) there is *little* job rotation between current team leaders and other team members.   [47] See Hernandez (1996).
[48] Such schemes typically involve transferring some decision making down to line workers.

to a large extent on the nature of tasks or decision rights that are being transferred upstream and downstream. If even a few complex tasks are being transferred downstream, top managers will have to deal with simpler problems and the move toward decentralization is likely to translate into a smaller revenue gap between the top management and the downstream units. Finally, segregation leads to more homogenous skill structures inside firms which mechanically reduces, in turn, wage inequality within any given enterprise.

Overall, *the impact of organizational change upon wage inequality comes out as highly ambiguous.* The move toward more organic firms may increase or reduce inequality, depending on whether polyvalence (and hence education) requirements overcome or not the consequences of despecialization and decision rights delegation induced by the flattening of organizations. Similarly, rising homogeneity of firms' skill structure will result in higher or lower inequality depending on the relative importance of across-firm effects (which enhance wage inequality) as compared to the within-firm effects (which tend to reduce it).

Our conjecture here is that the outcome of organizational change in terms of inequality heavily depends on the type of flexibility chosen by firms in the management of human resources. If relying on *external* flexibility, firms will react to any new need for human capital by firing unskilled workers and hiring skilled ones from the outside labor market. Such a strategy is bound to boost wage inequality across groups since it shifts the demand for skills upward. On the contrary, if firms rely on *internal* flexibility, they will choose to promote workers from the bottom end of the occupational or skill structure up to some higher layers. This may occur through formal training or rotation across jobs. The difference between both strategies is particularly clear when comparing the US and the UK, on the one hand, and Japan and Germany, on the other hand. In the former, flexibility is mainly external[49] while, in the latter, human capital accumulation inside firms is an important factor and internal flexibility thus plays a crucial role.[50] As underlined earlier in this subsection, wage

---

[49] See Lynch (1993) and Soskice (1993).   [50] See Koike (1988) and Marsden (1990).

inequality has sharply increased in the UK and the US since the early 1980s. This has not been the case in Japan, nor in Germany. We argue here that these diverging trends in inequality are likely to result from different choices regarding employment flexibility. More generally, we conjecture that flexibility strategies are important determinants of wage patterns in industrialized countries in particular, in that they condition the impact of organizational change upon wage inequality.

3.5 Discussion

We have seen in this section that growth and economic development do not necessarily entail a reduction in inequality, as the recent experience of OECD countries shows. Attempts to explain the increase in wage inequality have focused on trade, technological change, the evolution of labor-market institutions, and organizational change.

As economies develop and open to international trade, relative wages will change due to cross-country specialization. If industrialized economies have a relative advantage in skilled-labor-intensive goods, trading with developing countries will lead to further specialization in those goods. This induces a higher demand for skills and hence leads to a widening of the skilled–unskilled wage gap in these economies. Empirical tests of this hypothesis are based on measuring the shift in labor demand from unskilled-intensive industries to skilled-intensive ones, and show that only a negligible part of the shift away from unskilled to skilled labor in the US and the UK is due to *between*-industry changes, thereby appearing to refute the trade liberalization (or "globalization") explanation.

This evidence does not, however, imply that trade liberalization has played no role in the observed increase in the skill premium. In particular, a recent study showing evidence of a *substitution* between (imported) material inputs and unskilled labor across various industries in Germany, suggested to us that the skill-biased technical change and trade liberalization explanations might actually end up being *complementary*: namely, by lowering the cost of purchasing physical input – or by improving the variety (or mix) of physical inputs – trade liberalization may well be partly responsible for the observed change in the *direction* of technical change toward increasingly skill-demanding technologies even in sectors that do not directly trade with the south but yet are substituting material inputs for unskilled labor. This tentative hypothesis remains of course to be tested, in particular against alternative explanations.

Technical progress itself is one of the major engines of economic development. It is also an important source of inequality whenever it is not neutral, that is, if it affects differently the productivity of the various types of labor. We have seen that if new GPTs require skilled workers, their diffusion will increase inequality across educational groups. However, this rise is likely to be non-linear, because GPTs require social learning. In the first phase, the new technology diffuses slowly with almost no rise in wage inequality. In the second phase, on the contrary, its spreading accelerates and the skilled–unskilled wage gap widens. Finally, when the new GPT has been largely adopted, inequality decreases once more. The diffusion process thus results in a "temporary" Kuznets' curve during the transition from the old to the new GPT.

When embodied in capital vintages, technical progress enhances within-cohort inequality. We saw that, even if the productivity of a worker increases through learning-by-doing in any vintage, some reallocation of workers will take place toward new (and more productive) vintages as they arrive. The higher the rate of technical progress, the greater wage inequality across vintages is (as long as the former is over a certain threshold rate), first, because old technologies get obsolete faster and, second, because of a rising gap between the rate of productivity growth and that of learning-by-doing. However, this "growth effect" on inequality may be reversed by education. If education increases workers' mobility between vintages, as the rate of technical change rises more workers reallocate to new vintages and the productivity of those remaining on old lines increases due to the existence of decreasing returns. The overall impact on inequality will of course depend on the relative size of both effects.

The empirical evidence suggests that the weakening of labor-market institutions (deunionization, lowering of the minimum wage) has also contributed to widen both educational and occupational wage gaps. The crucial question that remains open is whether such changes are exogenous or whether they have occurred as a response to economic factors, such as the rise in unemployment and increased labor-market segmentation since the mid 1970s.

Be it embodied or not, technical progress stands as one important source of increasing inequality. Given that it is also the major force of economic growth, the Kuznets' hypothesis appears to be strongly challenged. It is all the more so that as technical change and human capital accumulate, firms organization gets modified. More organic structures develop, characterized by horizontal communication and task diversification. Organizations also become flatter and more homogenous with regard to skills. The impact of organizational change on wage inequality is ambiguous. On the one hand, organic firms require polyvalence, which increases the returns to skills. On the other hand, as decision rights are delegated downstream, firm owners need to avoid moral hazard. One way to do so is to raise wages in lower rank occupations, which reduces in turn occupational wage differentials. The distributional impact of organizational change thus remains undecided and is highly sensitive to the type of flexibility (internal or external) underlying human resources strategies.

On the whole, our analysis displays no evidence whatsoever that economic development should necessarily bring about a reduction in inequality. On the contrary, as long as technical progress is skill biased, technical, organizational, and trade effects go in the direction of a widening of wage inequality both across and within groups of workers. Hence, revisiting the Kuznets' hypothesis suggests that, if greater equality is to be a target of economic policy, it has to be tackled directly since market forces by themselves will, most likely, not do it all.

4 Conclusions

We have analyzed the relationship between inequality and economic growth from two directions. First, we have examined the effect of inequality on growth, showing that there is not necessarily a tradeoff between equality and efficiency. Second, we have addressed the impact that technological change has on wage inequality both across and within education cohorts.

An important policy implication that emerges from the first part of the survey is that, when capital markets are imperfect, there is scope for redistribution policies (transfers, subsidies to borrowers, public education, etc.) which are also growth enhancing. At the same time, education and the development of credit markets and institutions can help achieve long-lasting macroeconomic stability by reducing the separation between borrowers and investors, which, as we have seen, gives rise to macroeconomic fluctuations.

The extent to which education policy effectively reduces wage inequality when we allow for skill-biased technical change has been addressed in the second part of the survey. In the case of disembodied technical change, education narrows the differential between skilled and unskilled workers and has therefore the direct effect of reducing wage inequality. However, increasing the supply of skills has a counteracting impact on wage inequality because it is itself a cause of skill-biased technical change. Had there not been an initial mass of skilled labor, the (non-linear) implementation of new GPTs and changes in the direction of technical change toward skill-demanding technologies would not have taken place. The *long-run* effect of a greater stock of educated labor is consequently ambiguous. When technical change is embodied in capital goods, the effect of education on wage inequality is again ambiguous. On the one hand, education increases the mobility of workers across lines, helping them to catch-up from old to new vintages, and thus reducing the variance of wages across workers with similar initial skills. On the other hand, as pointed out by Lucas (1993), mobility enhances productivity growth and therefore increases the productivity gap between new and old vintages, thereby increasing wage inequality. This means that even in the *short run* the impact of education on the dispersion of wages is ambiguous.

The consequences of skill-biased technical change on inequality can, finally, be somewhat mitigated by organizational change, in particular by enhancing internal labor-market flexibility. Specifically, policies aimed at increasing firms' incentives to train and promote their existing workers (rather than competing in the hiring of already trained workers) in response to technological change, are likely to reduce the extent to which technological change increases wage inequality.

Appendix A1   Macroeconomic volatility

Consider an economy where there are two production technologies. The traditional technology uses only capital, so that output is given by $F_1(K) = \rho K$. The advanced technology uses both capital and labor according to $F_2(K,L) = K^\beta (AL)^{1-\beta}$. Let the level of technology be proportional to the stock of capital, so that the technology is AK. Normalizing the stock of labor to 1, we can express the wage and the interest rate in the advanced sector as $w = (1 - \beta)\sigma K$ and $r = \beta\sigma$, where σ is a constant. Assume that the traditional technology has a lower return than the advanced one, $\beta\sigma > \rho$. All individuals in the economy save a constant fraction of their wealth, s.

Two crucial assumptions are needed:

1 Inequality of access to investment: Only a fraction μ of savers can directly invest in high-yield projects.
2 Credit-market imperfections: An investor with wealth W can invest at most νW, where $\nu > 1$ is the credit multiplier.

Borrowing and lending take place at the beginning of a period. Because the interest rate is given, the lending market for high-yield projects need not clear. If the demand for savings is greater than the supply, all savings are invested in the high-yield technology and the interest rate is equal to $\beta\sigma$. If the demand for savings is less than the supply, some of the savings will be invested in the low-yield technology. The rate of interest will then be ρ. Production takes place. Wages and interest rates are received at the end of the period, and saving decisions are taken.

Let W_B^t and W_L^t denote the wealth of investors (borrowers) and non-investors (lenders). Total savings at the start of the period $t +$

1 are $S_t = W_B^t + W_L^t$. Total planned investment in the high-yield activity is given by $I_{t+1}^d = \nu W_B^t$.

The evolution of aggregate wealth depends on whether the economy is in an expansion or a recession. In a "boom" savings are less than desired investment, $S_t < I_{t+1}^d$, and all savings will be invested in the high-yield technology. The rate of growth of the economy will be $g^* = \log s + \log \sigma$, the highest possible. The wealth of borrowers and lenders next period will then be given by

$$W_B^{t+1} = s[\mu(1 - \beta)\sigma(W_B^t + W_L^t) + \beta\sigma(W_B^t + W_L^t) - \beta\sigma W_L^t] \qquad \text{(B)}$$

$$W_L^{t+1} = s[(1 - \mu)(1 - \beta)\sigma(W_B^t + W_L^t) + \beta\sigma W_L^t].$$

Since $W_B^t + W_L^t$ savings are invested in the high-yield activity during the boom, total output is $\sigma(W_B^t + W_L^t)$. The μ borrowers have two sources of income, labor income $(1 - \beta)\sigma(W_B^t + W_L^t)$ and the revenue from the investment activity $\beta\sigma(W_B^t + W_L^t)$. They have to pay an interest of $\beta\sigma$ on the amount borrowed, W_L^t. Lenders' income is composed of their labor income plus the interest received.

In a "slump" the demand for investment is smaller than total savings, $S_t > I_{t+1}^d$. In this case only a fraction of S_t is invested in the high-yield technology, the rest is employed in the low-yield technology. The interest rate in this case is ρ. Hence, next period's wealth of the two types of agents is given by

$$W_B^{t+1} = s[\mu(1 - \beta)\sigma\nu W_B^t + \beta\sigma\nu W_B^t - \rho(\nu - 1)W_B^t]$$
$$W_L^{t+1} = s[(1 - \mu)(1 - \beta)\sigma\nu W_B^t + \rho W_L^t]. \qquad \text{(S)}$$

Let $q^t = S_t / I_{t+1}^d$ be the ratio of savings over planned investment. Then, the two pairs of equations (B) and (S) can be combined to obtain two difference equations that describe the evolution of q^t over time. When the economy is in a boom at the beginning of period $t + 1$, that is when $q^t < 1$, we have

$$q^{t+1} = \left[a + b\frac{1}{q_t} \right]^{-1} \qquad \text{(B')}$$

and when it is in a slump, that is when $q^t > 1$, we have

$$q^{t+1} = c + dq^t \qquad \text{(S')}$$

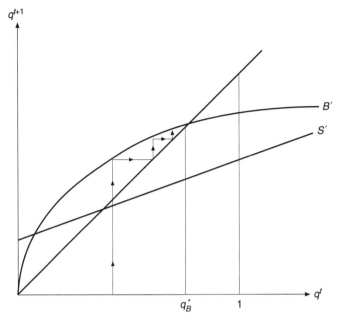

Figure A1

where the constants a, b, c, and d are all positive and such that $1/(a+b) > c+d$.

The two dynamic equations (B') and (S') define a system that can be represented graphically. Both functions are increasing and cut the 45°-line from above. Note also that the (B') curve lies above the (S') curve for $q^t = 1$. There are then three possible situations.

1 Permanent boom: Figure A1 depicts the case where the equilibria are such that $1 > q_B^* > q_S^*$. This condition is satisfied whenever $1 > q_B^* = (1 - b)/a$, which can be shown to be equivalent to

$$\mu \cdot \nu > 1.$$

If the number of individuals with direct investment opportunities is large relative to the degree of credit-market imperfection, the economy will be on a high-growth path. In the absence of credit-market

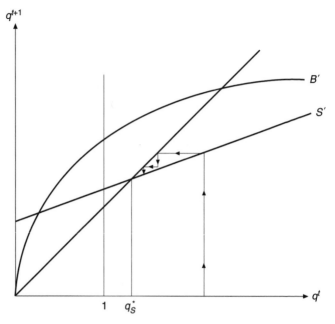

Figure A2

imperfection ($\nu \to \infty$) or of inequality of opportunities ($\mu = 1$) the above condition is always satisfied.

2 Permanent slump: Figure A2 depicts the case where the equilibria are such that $1 < q_S^* < q_B^*$. This condition is satisfied whenever $1 < q_S^* = c/(1-d)$, which can be shown to be equivalent to

$$\mu < \frac{1}{1-\beta} \left(\frac{\sigma - \rho}{\sigma} \frac{1}{\nu} - \frac{\beta \sigma - \rho}{\sigma} \right).$$

Permanent slumps tend to occur when the credit multiplier is small (ν low) and/or few people have direct access to the high-yield technology (μ low).

3 Cycles: Figure A3 corresponds to the case where $q_S^* < 1 < q_B^*$. The economy exhibits cycles, moving back and forth from booms to slumps. Cycles occur whenever

$$\frac{1}{\nu} > \mu > \frac{1}{1-\beta} \left(\frac{\sigma - \rho}{\sigma} \frac{1}{\nu} - \frac{\beta \sigma - \rho}{\sigma} \right).$$

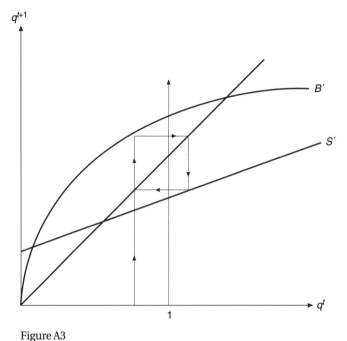

Figure A3

Both in a permanent-slump equilibrium and in a cyclical one the rate of growth will be below its potential level, g^*.

Appendix A2 Political economy

Individuals are endowed with different amounts of human capital, given by $w_t^i = \epsilon_t^i \cdot A_t$. Production of future consumption good takes place according to the AK-technology $y_t^i = (k_t^i)^\alpha (A_t)^{1-\alpha}$, where $A_t = y_{t-1}$. Following Benabou (1996), consider the following log-linear investment tax scheme, whereby an individual with pre-tax investment k^i ends up with the post-tax investment

$$k^i(\tau) = (k^i)^{1-\tau} \cdot (\tilde{k})^\tau,$$

where $\tilde{k}$ is the average investment. If we express investments in logarithms, the above equation implies a linear tax scheme such as the one described in subsection 2.4, $\log k^i(\tau) = (1-\tau)\log k^i + \tau$

log k. This formulation of the tax-benefit system makes it easier to find an analytical solution, although the results are the same as with a linear tax system, $k^i(\tau) = (1 - \tau)k^i + \tau k$ (see Persson and Tabellini 1994).

Assume that there are no credit constraints. Expecting the investment tax rate τ, individual i solves the following problem

$$\max_{b^i, k^i}\{\ln(w^i + b^i - k^i) + \rho\ln(\overbrace{(k^i(\tau))^\alpha w^{1-\alpha} - rb^i}^{=y^i})\}$$

The first-order condition for this maximization, together with the loan market-clearing condition $\int_0^1 b^i di = 0$, yields the investment and net borrowing decisions

$$k^i = \frac{\rho\alpha(1 - \tau)}{1 + \rho\alpha(1 - \tau)} \cdot w \quad \text{and} \quad b^i = \frac{\rho}{1 + \rho}(w - w^i),$$

where $s(\tau) = \rho\alpha(1 - \tau)/(1 + \rho\alpha(1 - \tau))$ is the saving rate. The saving rate is the same for all individuals and is decreasing in the tax rate. In the AK-model, the rate of growth is determined by the saving rate. The growth rate during period t is $g_t = \ln y_t/y_{t-1}$. That is

$$g_t = \ln\frac{A_t^{1-\alpha}\int_0^1(k_t^i)^\alpha di}{A_t},$$

where $k_t^i = s(\tau)w_t$. We can then express it simply as $g_t = \alpha\ln s(\tau)$. Since the saving rate is decreasing in τ, the incentive effect implies that growth is higher when redistribution is lowest.

In order to examine how τ is determined we calculate the indirect utility function for individual i

$$U^i(\tau) = V(\tau) + G(w^i/w,\tau),$$

where $V(\tau)$ is the intertemporal utility of the individual with wealth equal to the average w, who in this case is also the individual with average investment $\tilde{k}$, and $G(w^i/w,\tau)$ is an individual specific term. The intertemporal utility of the agent with average wealth is

$$V(\tau) = \ln(w - k) + \rho\ln(k^\alpha w^{1-\alpha})$$
$$= (1 + \rho)\ln w + \ln(1 - s(\tau)) + \rho\alpha\ln(s(\tau)),$$

and the individual specific term is given by

$$G(w^i/w,\tau) = (1 + \rho)\ln\left[1 + \frac{w^i/w - 1}{(1 + \rho)(1 - s(\tau))}\right].$$

$V(\tau)$ is decreasing with τ as a result of the negative *incentive* effect of redistribution. $G(w^i/w,\tau)$ is such that

$$\partial G/\partial \tau \begin{cases} < 0 \text{ for } w^i > w \\ = 0 \text{ for } w^i = w \\ > 0 \text{ for } w^i < w \end{cases}$$

The preferred tax rate of each individual is given by the first-order condition $\partial U^i(\tau)/\partial \tau = 0$. It is implicitly defined by

$$\frac{\tau^*(1 + \rho)}{(1 + \rho(1 - \tau^*))(1 + \rho\alpha(1 - \tau^*))} = 1 - \frac{w^i}{w}.$$

It is straightforward to show that the resulting preferred tax rate of individual i, $\tau^*(w^i,\rho,\alpha)$, is decreasing in w^i.

Appendix A3 Appropriability of knowledge and the effects of technical change on wage inequality: a toy vintage model

This appendix draws unrestrainedly upon current work with Peter Howitt and GianLuca Violante.

We consider a simple discrete time/infinite horizon model of technical change, learning-by-doing, and frictional labor reallocations in which:

(1) *Technical knowledge* is embodied in capital of increasing vintage over time. The productivity gap between two successive vintages is measured by some parameter γ. And we assume that every period a new vintage is being introduced and that firms that adopt this new vintage live only for two periods. (The parameter γ will thus also measure the rate of productivity growth.)

Thus, at any date t, there are only two lines (or vintages) in operation: vintage t and vintage $t-1$; or equivalently, the new vintage (of age 0) and the old vintage (of age 1).

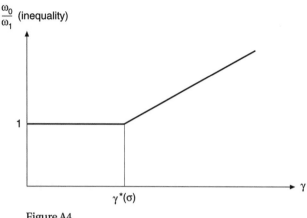

Figure A4

(2) *Labor-market frictions* are modelled as follows: only a fraction σ at most of workers currently working on a (old) line, get the opportunity to move to the leading edge. Those workers who get such an opportunity may still decide not to "exercise" it and instead to remain on their current line. Let N_{ij}^t denote the (current) flow of workers from age i on line $(t-1)$ to age j on line t, where $(i,j) \epsilon \{0,1\}^2$ (a worker cannot stay more than two periods on a given line); and let $N_{t,i}$ (resp. $N_{t-1,i}$) denote the number of workers on line of age i at date t (resp. $t-1$).

The flows of workers are depicted in figure A4. Thus the labor flows $N_{1,1}$ and $N_{0,0}$ refer to *movers*, whilst $N_{1,0}$ and $N_{0,1}$ refer to *workers who stay*, i.e., respectively of age 1 on old vintage firms, who then automatically relocated to leading-edge vintage next period ($N_{1,0}$), and of age 0 on new vintage which remain on some vintage next period (N_{01}).

(3) *Learning -by-doing* on each vintage takes place at rate η, and generates knowledge that is appropriated either by firms or by workers on that vintage. We shall assume that $\gamma > \eta$, i.e., a young firm (or worker) on a new technology is more efficient "ceteris paribus" than an experienced firm (or worker) with an old technology.

(4) Workers are infinitely lived, have linear preferences (so that they only care about NPV of wage incomes), and discount the future at rate β.

We are primarily interested by the effects of growth (i.e., of γ) on wage inequality under alternative assumptions, first, on the *appropriability* of knowledge between firms and workers, and, second, on the *transferability* of (workers') knowledge from old to new vintages (as a function of the "technological distance" between the old and the new vintage).

A3.1 The case where firms appropriate all the learning-by-doing-generated knowledge.[51]

We concentrate on a steady-state equilibrium in which $N_{i,t} \equiv N_i$ and $N_{i,t-1} \equiv N_i$. Consider now any date t; the output flow of firms of age 0 (respectively of age 1) is given by

$$Y_{t0} = A_t \underbrace{(N_{00} + N_{10})}_{N_0}{}^{\alpha},$$

where $A_t = (1 + \gamma)^t$ and $0 < \alpha < 1$

$$(\text{resp. } Y_{t1} = (1 + \eta)A_{t-1}\underbrace{(N_{01} + N_{11})}_{N_1}{}^{\alpha}).$$

Productivity – adjusted wages for workers on lines of age 0 and 1 are then simply equal to

$$\omega_0 = \frac{w_{t0}}{A_t} = \alpha(N_{10} + N_{00})^{\alpha - 1}$$

$$\text{and } \omega_1 = \frac{w_{t1}}{A_t} = \frac{1 + \eta}{1 + \gamma}\alpha(N_{01} + N_{11})^{\alpha - 1} \tag{W}$$

Now let V_0 (resp. V_1) denote the productivity-adjusted value for a worker to be currently on a line of age 0 (resp. 1) until a new

---

[51] This is the case analyzed in section 2.2.2 above.

relocation opportunity comes up. The Bellman equations defining V_0 and V_1, can be expressed as

$$V_0 = \omega_0 + \beta \sigma^*(1 + \gamma) V_0 + \beta (1 - \sigma^*)(1 + \gamma) V_1 \quad \text{(A1)}$$

$$V_1 = \omega_1 + \beta \sigma^*(1 + \gamma) V_0 + \beta(1 - \sigma^*)(1 + \gamma) V_0, \quad \text{(A2)}$$

where: β is the discount factor; σ^* is the actual probability of relocation ($\sigma^* \leq \sigma$ and $\sigma^* < \sigma$ iff $V_0 = V_1$); and $(1 + \gamma) V_i$ is the productivity-adjusted value of being on a line of age i next period.[52]

From (A1) and (A2), it follows immediately that

$$V_1 - V_0 = \frac{\omega_1 - \omega_0}{1 + \delta(1 - \sigma^*)} \quad \text{(A3)}$$

Definition: A stationary equilibrium is a vector $\{\sigma^*, \omega_1^*, \omega_0^*\}$ such that:

(E1) $N_{01} = N_{10}$ (so that $N_{11} = 0$)
(E2) $\sigma^* \leq \sigma$, with $\sigma^* < \sigma$ whenever $V_1 = V_0$
(E3) $N_{00} = \sigma^*(N_{00} + N_{10})$, where $N_{00} + N_{10} = N_0$ and N_0 is the initial number of workers on a new vintage.

Now, we can easily solve for the stationary equilibrium and thereby for the equilibrium wage ratio ω_0 / ω_1 as a function of the rate of productivity growth, γ.

Let $\bar{N} = N_{01} = N_{10}$. We then have:

$$N_{00} = \frac{\sigma^*}{1 - \sigma^*} \bar{N},$$

and therefore, using (W)

$$\Rightarrow \frac{\omega_{t0}}{\omega_{t1}} = \frac{\omega_0}{\omega_1}(\sigma^*) = \frac{1 + \gamma}{1 + \eta}(1 - \sigma^*)^{1-\alpha},$$

---

[52] In words, a worker currently on a line of age 0 either relocates to the new leading-edge tomorrow (with probability σ^*) or he/she remains on the same line which will then be of age 1. Hence equation (A1). On the other hand, a worker currently on a line of age 1 will always relocate on the new leading-edge technology when his/her current line becomes obsolete next period. This, in turn, follows, first, from our assumption that firms cannot live for more than two periods and, second, from the fact that $N_{11} = 0$ in a stationary equilibrium (see below).

where:

(a) $\sigma^* < \sigma$ if, conditional upon *all* upgraded workers actually relocating to the newest vintage, V_0 ended up being strictly lower than V_1 or equivalently (by (A3)), if

$$\frac{\omega_0}{\omega_1}(\sigma) = \frac{1 + \gamma}{1 + \eta}(1 - \sigma)^{1-\alpha} < 1.$$

The equilibrium relocation rate σ^* is then simply defined by

$$\frac{1 + \gamma}{1 + \eta}(1 - \sigma^*) = 1$$

and there is no wage inequality in equilibrium.

(b) $\sigma^* = \sigma$ if

$$\frac{1 + \gamma}{1 + \eta}(1 - \sigma^*)^{1-\alpha} \geq 1.$$

Now, we can look at wage inequality as a function of γ. As γ increases, the economy shifts from the non-frictional labor-market regime ($\sigma^* < \sigma$), where there is no wage inequality, to the frictional regime ($\sigma^* = \sigma$), where inequality is positive and increases with γ, as depicted in figure A5 below. (This figure is not surprisingly similar to figure 12).

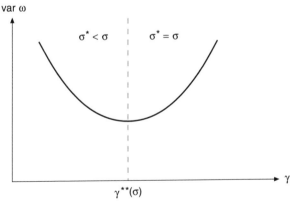

Figure A5

where $\gamma^*(\sigma)$ is defined by: $\frac{1 + \gamma^*}{1 + \eta}(1 - \sigma)^{1-\alpha} = 1.$

A3.2 *The case where workers appropriate the knowledge.*

In this case the output flow of firms of age 0 is of the form:

$$Y_{t0} = A_t \cdot (q_{00}N_{00} + q_{10}N_{10})^\alpha,$$

where we still assume that $A_t = (1 + \gamma)^t$ and $0 < \alpha < 1$, and where q_{ij} denotes the *quality* of a worker that just moved from a line of age i into a line of age j. For firms of age 1 we have

$$Y_{t1} = A_{t-1}(q_{01}N_{01} + q_{11}N_{11})^\alpha = A_{t-1}(q_{01}N_{01})^\alpha$$

in a stationary equilibrium where we know that $N_{11} \equiv 0$.

Then, if ω_{ij} denotes the productivity-adjusted wage of a type (i,j) worker that just moved from a line of age i into a line of age j, we have

$$\omega_{00} = \alpha(q_{00}N_{00} + q_{10}N_{10})^{\alpha-1} \cdot q_{00}$$

$$\omega_{10} = \alpha(q_{00}N_{00} + q_{10}N_{10})^{\alpha-1} \cdot q_{10} \qquad \text{(W)}$$

$$\omega_{01} = \alpha(q_{01}N_{01})^{\alpha-1} q_{10} \cdot \frac{1}{1+\gamma}$$

(the wage ω_{11} is irrelevant since $N_{11} \equiv 0$ in a stationary equilibrium).

The main difference with the previous case is that now different types of workers on lines of age 0 will get different wages, since knowledge is worker specific instead of being purely vintage specific: $\omega_{00} \neq \omega_{10}$.

In the same way as before, a stationary equilibrium is defined as a vector $(\sigma^*, \omega_{00}^*, \omega_{10}^*, \omega_{01}^*)$ such that:

(E1) $N_{10} = N_{01}$ and $N_{11} = 0$
(E2) $\sigma^* \leq \sigma$, with $\sigma^* < \sigma$ whenever $V_{01} = V_{00}$ or equivalently when $\omega_{01} = \omega_{00}$.
(E3) $N_{00} = \sigma^*(N_{00} + N_{10})$,

where V_{ij} is the value of a type (i,j) worker until an upgrading opportunity comes up.

Learning-by-doing assumptions: We assume

$$q_{00} = 1 + \eta\bar{\tau},$$
$$q_{01} = 1 + \eta,$$
$$q_{10} = 1 + \eta\underline{\tau},$$

where $0 < \underline{\tau} < \bar{\tau} < 1$, and $\eta > 0$.

In other words, whilst type $(0,1)$ workers that have remained on the same line for one period already can fully take advantage of learning-by-doing (equation (Q2)), other types of worker that have just arrived on their current line will not be as productive (i.e., $\underline{\tau}$ and $\bar{\tau}$, are less than 1 in equations Q1 and Q3); and the further away they come, the less productive they initially are (this "transferability of knowledge" assumption we capture by the inequality $\underline{\tau} < \bar{\tau}$).

Let us now solve for stationary equilibrium and then determine the evolution of wage inequality as a function of γ.

As before, if $\bar{N} = N_{01} = N_{10}$, we have

$$N_{00} = \frac{\sigma^*}{1 - \sigma^*} \bar{N}.$$

Thus, from the wage equations (W)

$$\underbrace{\frac{\omega_{00}}{\omega_{01}}(\sigma^*) = (1 + \gamma)\left[\frac{q_{00}\sigma^* + q_{10}(1 - \sigma^*)}{q_{01}(1 - \sigma^*)}\right]^{\alpha - 1} \cdot \frac{q_{00}}{q_{01}}}_{\varphi(\gamma, \sigma^*)}.$$

As before, the relocation constraint $\sigma^* \leq \sigma$ will be binding (i.e., $\sigma^* = \sigma$) whenever $\frac{\omega_{00}}{\omega_{01}}(\sigma) = \varphi(\gamma, \sigma^*) \geq 1$, otherwise the equilibrium relocation rate $\sigma^* < \sigma$ is determined by: $\varphi(\gamma, \sigma^*) = 1$.

As γ varies from 0 to $+\infty$, given that $\varphi(\gamma, \sigma)$ is increasing in γ and decreasing in σ, the economy will successively go through a non-frictional and then a frictional labor-market regime, as shown in figure A6 below. But unlike in the case where firms appropriate all the knowledge, here wage inequality obtains even for low values of γ. When $\sigma^* < \sigma$ and therefore $\omega_{00} = \omega_{01}$, we still have

$$\frac{\omega_{00}}{\omega_{01}} = \frac{q_{10}}{q_{00}} = \frac{1 + \eta\underline{\tau}}{1 + \eta\bar{\tau}} < 1.$$

If we measure wage inequality by the wage variance: $var(\omega) = E(\omega - \bar{\omega})^2$, where $\bar{\omega} = E\omega$, then we can establish:

Proposition A3.1: *Let $\gamma^{**}(\sigma)$ denote the cut-off productivity-growth rate defined by $\varphi(\gamma^{**}(\sigma), \sigma) = 1$. Then (a) a small increase in γ in the non-frictional region $\gamma < \gamma^{**}(\sigma)$ will have the unambiguous effect of reducing inequality; (b) a small increase in γ in*

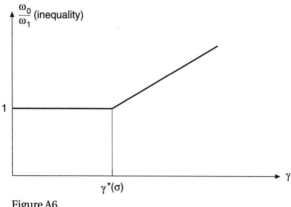

Figure A6

the *frictional region* $\gamma > \gamma^{**}(\sigma)$ *results in an* increase *in wage* inequality.

We thus obtain the picture shown in figure A6.

Proof of Proposition A3.1:
(a) Note that the equilibrium relocation rate σ^* is an increasing function of γ for $\gamma < \gamma^{**}(\sigma)$. (This follows from the fact that the function $\varphi(\gamma, \hat{\sigma})$ is increasing in γ and decreasing in $\hat{\sigma}$ and from the fact that σ^* is implicitly defined by: $\varphi(\gamma, \sigma^*) = 1$.

Note also that as σ^* increases, the ratio between the number of workers on the newest line and the number of workers on the old line

$$\frac{N_{00} + N_{01}}{N_{10}} = \frac{\dfrac{\sigma^*}{1 - \sigma^*} + 1}{1} = \frac{1}{1 - \sigma^*}$$

is indeed increasing in σ^*. Now, part (a) follows straightforwardly from the fact that, for $\gamma < \gamma^{**}(\sigma), \omega_{01} = \omega_{00}$, and therefore

$$var(\omega) = \frac{N_{00} + N_{01}}{N_{10}} (\omega_{00} - \bar{\omega})^2 + \frac{N_{10}}{N} (\omega_{10} - \bar{\omega})^2$$

where $N = N_{00} + N_{01} + N_{10}$ is the total size of the labor force and $\bar{\omega}$ is the average wage

$$\bar{\omega} = \frac{N_{00} + N_{01}}{N}\omega_{00} + \frac{N_{10}}{N}\omega_{10}.$$

Thus, as γ and therefore σ^* increases, the wage distribution moves closer to perfect equality at ω_{00}.

More precisely, we have

$$var(\omega) = \frac{1-\sigma^*}{(2-\sigma^*)^2}(\omega_{10} - \omega_{00})^2.$$

Part (a) then follows from the fact that: (i): the function $\frac{1-\sigma^*}{(2-\sigma^*)^2}$ is decreasing in σ^* and (ii)

$$\omega_{10} - \omega_{10} = \alpha(q_{00} - q_{10})(q_{00}N_{00} + q_{10}N_{10})^{\alpha-1}$$

$$= \alpha(\eta\tau - \eta\tau')((1+\eta\tau)\frac{\sigma^*}{(2-\sigma^*)} + (1+\eta\tau')\frac{1-\sigma^*}{2-\sigma^*})^{\alpha-1}$$

which is also decreasing in σ^* since $\tau > \tau'$ and $\alpha < 1$.

(Intuitively, an increase in γ stimulates workers' reallocation to the new vintage which in turn reduces wage inequality, both because more workers earn the same wage ω_{00} and because of decreasing returns to labor on each line, including new lines.)

(b) When $\gamma > \gamma^{**}(\sigma)$, we have

$$var(\omega) = \frac{N_{00}}{N}(\omega_{00} - \bar{\omega})^2 + \frac{N_{01}}{N}(\omega_{01} - \bar{\omega})^2 + \frac{N_{10}}{N}(\omega_{10} - \bar{\omega})^2,$$

where $N_{00}, N_{01}, N_{10}, \omega_{00}$, and ω_{10} are now independent of γ since $\sigma^* \equiv \sigma$ and the qs are also independent of γ.

Thus, an increase in γ only has the effect of reducing the relative wage of workers on the old line which was already lower than the wages of workers on the new line. It therefore increases the overall amount of wage inequality.

References

Acemoglu, D. 1996. "Changes in Unemployment and Wage Inequality: An Alternative Theory and Some Evidence." CEPR discussion paper 1459.

———. 1997. "Why Do New Technologies Complement Skills? Directed Technical Change and Wage Inequality." CEPR working paper.

Acemoglu, D. and Newman, A. 1997. "The Labor Market and Corporate Structure." Mimeo, MIT.

Aghion, P., Banerjee, A., and Piketty, T. 1997. "Dualism and Macroeconomic Volatility." Mimeo, University College London.

Aghion, P. and Bolton, P. 1997. "A Trickle-Down Theory of Growth and Development with Debt Overhang." *Review of Economic Studies*, 64: 151–162.

Aghion, P. and Howitt, P. 1998. *Endogenous Growth Theory*. MIT Press.

Aghion, P. and Tirole, J. 1997. "Formal and Real Authority in Organizations." *Journal of Political Economy*, 105(1): 1–29.

Alesina, A. and Perotti, R. 1996. "Income Distribution, Political Instability, and Investment." *European Economic Review*, 40: 1203–1228.

Alesina, A. and Rodrik, D. 1994. "Distributive Politics and Economic Growth." *Quarterly Journal of Economics*, 109: 465–490.

Atkinson, A. (1996): "Bringing Income Distribution in from the Cold," Presidential Address to the Royal Economic Society, Swansea.

Benabou, R. 1996. "Inequality and Growth," *NBER Macroeconomics Annual.*

Berman, E., Bound, J., and Griliches, Z. 1994. "Changes in Demand for Skilled Labor within US Manufacturing: Evidence from the Annual Survey of Manufactures." *Quarterly Journal of Economics*, 109: 367–397.

Bolton, P. and Dewatripont, M. 1994. "The Firm as a Communication Network." *Quarterly Journal of Economics*, 4: 809–839.

Borjas, G. J., Freeman, R.B., and Katz, L. F. 1992. "On the Labor Market Effects of Immigration and Trade." In G. J. Borjas and R. B. Freeman (eds.), *Immigration and the Workforce: Economic Consequences for the United States and Source Areas*. Chicago University Press, Chicago.

Bound, J. and Johnson, G. 1992. "Changes in the Structure of Wages in the 1980's: An Evaluation of Alternative Explanations." *American Economic Review*, 82(3): 371–392.

Cappelli, P. and Daniel, K. 1995. "Technology, Work Organization and the Structure of Wages." Working paper, University of Pennsylvania, Wharton.

Card, D. 1992: "The Effect of Unions on the Distribution of Wages: Redistribution or Relabelling." NBER working paper 4195.

Card, D. and Krueger, A. 1995. *Myth and Measurement: The New Economics of the Minimum Wage.* Princeton University Press, Princeton.

Caroli, E. and Van Reenen, J. 1997. "Human Capital and Organizational Change: Evidence from British Establishments in the 1980s." Mimeo, University College London.

Caroli, E., Greenan, N., and Guellec, D. 1997. "Organizational Change and Human Capital Accumulation." Mimeo, CEPREMAP.

David, P. (1990): "The Computer and the Dynamo: An Historical Perspective on the Productivity Paradox," *American Economic Review,* 80 (May), 355–361.

DiNardo, J., Fortin, N., and Lemieux, T. 1996. "Labor Market Institutions and the Distribution of Wages 1973–1992: A Semi-Parametric Approach." *Econometrica,* 65: 1001–1044.

Falk, M. and Koebel, B. 1997. "The Demand for Heterogeneous Labour in Germany." Zentrum fur Europaische Wirtschaftsforschung GmbH discussion paper 97–28, Mannheim.

Fortin, N. and Lemieux, T. 1997. "Institutional Changes and Rising Wage Inequality: Is there a Linkage?" *Journal of Economic Perspectives,* 11(2): 75–96.

Freeman, R. 1993. "How Much Has Deunionization Contributed to the Rise in Male Earnings Inequality?" In Danziger, S. Sheldon, and Gottschalk, P. (eds.), *Uneven Tides: Rising Inequality in America.* Russell Sage Foundation, New-York, pp. 133–163.

Galor, O. and Tsiddon, D. (1994): "Human Capital Distribution, Technological Progress, and Economic Growth." Mimeo, Brown University.

Galor, O. and Zeira, J. 1993. "Income Distribution and Macroeconomics." *Review of Economic Studies,* 60: 35–52.

García-Peñalosa, C. 1995. "The Paradox of Education or the Good Side of Inequality." *Oxford Economic Papers,* 47: 265–285.

———— 1996. "Trade and Skill-Biased Technical Change." Mimeo, Nuffield College, Oxford.

Glomm, G. and Ravikumar, B. 1992: "Public vs Private Investment in Human Capital: Endogenous Growth and Income Inequality." *Journal of Political Economy,* 4: 818–834.

Gosling, A. and Machin, S. 1995. "Trade Unions and the Dispersion of Earnings in British Establishments 1980–90." *Oxford Bulletin of Economics and Statistics,* 57: 161–184.

Gosling, A., Machin, S., and Meghir, C. 1995. "What has Happened to Men's Wages since the Mid-1960s?" *Fiscal Studies,* 15: 63–87.

Hausmann, R. and Gavin, M. 1996a. "Determinants of Macroeconomic Volatility in Developing Economies." Mimeo, Inter-American Development Bank.

 1996b. "Securing Stability and Growth in a Shock-Prone Region: The Policy Challenges for Latin America." In Hausmann, R. and Reisen, H. (eds.) *Securing Stability and Growth in Latin America.* OECD, Paris.

Hernandez, F. 1996. "Essays on the Economics of Corporate Control: Applications to Internal Labor Markets and Corporate Finance." Nuffield College, Oxford University Ph.D. dissertation.

Juhn, C., Murphy, K., and Pierce, B. 1993. "Wage Inequality and the Rise in Returns to Skill." *Journal of Political Economy*, 101(3): 410–442.

Katz, L. F., and Murphy, K. M. 1992. "Changes in Relative Wages, 1963–1987: Supply and Demand Factors." *Quarterly Journal of Economics*, 107: 35–78.

Koebel, B. 1997. "Aggregation in Production Analysis: Heterogeneity and Representativity." Ph.D. Thesis, Louis Pasteur University, Strasbourg.

Koike, K. 1988. *Understanding Industrial Relations in Modern Japan.* St Martin's Press, New York.

Kramarz, F. 1997. "International Competition, Employment and Wages: The Microeconometrics of International Trade." CEPR working paper.

Kremer, M., and Maskin, E. 1996. "Wage Inequality and Segregation by Skill." NBER working paper 5718.

Krueger, A. 1993 "How Computers have Changed the Wage Structure." *The Quarterly Journal of Economics*, 108: 33–60.

Krugman, P. 1995. "Growing World Trade: Causes and Consequences." *Brookings Papers on Economic Activity*, 327–362.

 1998. "What Happened to Asia?" Mimeo, MIT.

Krusell, P., Ohanian, L., Rios-Rull, J-V., and Violante, G. L. 1996. "Capital-Skill Complementarity and Inequality." Mimeo, University of Rochester.

Kuznets, S. 1955. "Economic Growth and Income Inequality." *American Economic Review*, 45: 1–28.

Lawrence, R. Z. and Slaughter, M. J. 1993. "International Trade and American Wages in the 1980s: Giant Sucking Sound or Small Hiccup?" *Brookings Papers on Economic Activity*, 161–210.

Legros, P. and Newman, A. 1994. "Wealth Effects, Distribution, and the Theory of Organization." Mimeo, Cornell and Columbia Universities.

Lindbeck, A. and Snower, D. 1996. "Reorganization of Firms and Labor Market Inequality." CEPR Discussion paper 1375.

Lucas, R. E. 1988. "On the Mechanics of Economic Development." *Journal of Monetary Economics*, 22(1): 3–42.

1993. "Making a Miracle." *Econometrica*, 61: 251–272.

Lynch, L. 1993. "The Economics of Youth Training in the United-States." *The Economic Journal*, 103(420): 1292–1302.

Machin, S. 1995. "Changes in the Relative Demand for Skills." In A.L. Booth and D. Snower (eds.), *Acquiring Skills. Market Failures, their Symptoms and Policy Responses.* Cambridge University Press.

1996. "Wage Inequality in the UK." *Oxford Review of Economic Policy*, 12(1): 47–64.

1997a. "The decline of Labor Market Institutions and the Rise in Wage Inequality in Britain." *European Economic Review*, 41: 647–657.

1997b. "What Explains the Deterioration of the Labor Market Position of the Unskilled?" Mimeo, London School of Economics.

Machin, S. and Manning, A. 1994. "Minimum Wages, Wage Dispersion and Employment: Evidence from the UK Wages Council." *Industrial and Labor Relations Review*, 47: 319–329.

Marsden, D. 1990. "Institutions and Labor Mobility: Occupational and Internal Labor Markets in Britain, France, Italy and West-Germany." In Brunetta, R. and Dell'Aringa, C. (eds.), *Labor Relations and Economic Performance.* MacMillan, London, pp. 414–438.

Mirrlees, J. 1971. "An Exploration in the Theory of Optimum Income Taxation." *Review of Economic Studies*, 38: 175–208.

Mishel, L., Bernstein, J. and Schmitt, J. 1996. *The State of Working America 1996–97.* ME Sharpe, New York.

Murphy, K. and Welch, F. 1992. "The Structure of Wages." *Quarterly Journal of Economics*, 107: 285–326.

Nickell, S. J. and Bell, B. 1995. "The Collapse in Demand for the Unskilled and Unemployment across the OECD." *Oxford Review of Economic Policy*, 11(1): 40–62.

OECD. 1993. *Employment Outlook.*

Owens, T. and Wood, A. 1997. "Export-Oriented Industrialization Through Primary Processing?" *World Development*, 25: 1453–1470.

Perotti, R. 1993. "Political Equilibrium, Income Distribution, and Growth." *Review of Economic Studies*, 60: 755–776.

1996. "Growth, Income Distribution, and Democracy: What the Data Say." *Journal of Economic Growth*, 1: 149–187.

Persson, T. and Tabellini, G. 1994. "Is Inequality Harmful for Growth?" *American Economic Review*, 84(3): 600–621.

Piketty, T. (1996): "Inegalites et Redistribution." *Revue d'Economie Politique*, 104(6): 769–800.

Piore, M. 1988. "Corporate Reform in American Manufacturing and the Challenge to Economic Theory." MIT working paper 533.

Rebelo, S. 1991. "Long-Run Policy Analysis and Long-Run Growth." *Journal of Political Economy,* 99 (June): 500–521.

Revenga, A.L. 1992. "Exporting Jobs?" *The Quarterly Journal of Economics,* 107: 255–284.

Sachs, J. D. and Shatz, H. J. 1994. "Trade and Jobs in US Manufacturing." *Brookings Papers on Economic Activity.* 1–69.

Saint-Paul, G. and Verdier, T. 1993. "Education, Democracy and Growth." *Journal of Development Economics,* 42(2): 399–407.

Scott, E., O'Shaugnessy, K., and Cappelli, P. 1996. "Management Jobs in the Insurance Industry: Organization, Deskilling and Rising Pay Inequality." Working paper, University of Pennsylvania, Wharton.

Shleifer, A. 1986. "Implementation Cycles." *Journal of Political Economy,* 94: 1163–1190.

Soskice, D. 1993. "Social Skills from Mass Higher Education: Rethinking the Company-Based Initial Training Paradigm." *Oxford Review of Economic Policy,* 9(3): 101–113.

Stiglitz, J.E. 1969. "The Distribution of Income and Wealth Among Individuals." *Econometrica,* 37(3): 382–397.

Stole, L., and Zwiebel, J. 1996. "Intra-Firm Bargaining under Non-Binding Contracts." *Review of Economic Studies,* 63: 375–410.

Tamura, R. 1991. "Income Convergence in an Endogenous Growth Model." *Journal of Political Economy,* 99(3): 522–540.

Violante, G. L. 1996. "Equipment Investment and Skill Dynamics: A Solution to the Wage Dispersion Puzzle?" Mimeo, University College, London.

Wood, A. 1994. *North-South Trade, Employment and Inequality: Changing Fortunes in a Skill Driven World.* Clarendon Press, Oxford.

Wood, A. and Ridao-Cano, C. 1996. "Skill, Trade and International Inequality." Working paper 46, Institute of Development Studies.

PART TWO

Globalization and the labor market: using history to inform policy

Jeffrey G. Williamson

ONE

Globalization, labor markets and convergence in the past

1.1 Globalization, convergence, and history

Two important features of the world economy since 1970 also characterized the world economy a century ago. First, the earlier period was one of rapid globalization: capital and labor flowed across national frontiers in unprecedented quantities, and commodity trade boomed in response to sharply declining transport costs. Second, the late nineteenth century underwent an impressive convergence in living standards, at least within most of what we would now call the OECD, but what historians call the Atlantic economy. Poor countries around the European periphery tended to grow faster than the rich industrial leaders at the European center, and often even faster than the labor-scarce countries overseas in the New World. This Atlantic economy excluded, of course, Asia, Africa, the Middle East, and Eastern Europe. There were also some who failed to catch up even around the exclusive Atlantic economy periphery, but they were few.

A recent literature has developed which argues that most of the convergence between 1850 and 1914 was due to the open

This chapter draws heavily on my own previous work (Williamson 1995, 1996) and that with Kevin O'Rourke (O'Rourke and Williamson 1997a, 1997b). I gratefully acknowledge the collaboration with Professor O'Rourke, and his generous permission to allow me to draw on our joint work for this lecture.

economy forces of trade and mass migration. By inference, it also suggests that convergence stopped between 1914 and 1950 because of de-globalization and implosion into autarchy. These facts are directly relevant to debates over globalization today. This revisionist historical research also shows that these globalization forces had an important distributional impact within participating countries. Perhaps most importantly, it suggests that these distributional events helped create a globalization backlash which caused a drift toward more restrictive immigration and tariff policy prior to World War I. These chapters will visit all of these issues. This first of the three chapters, however, will document the globalization of the participants' labor markets, real wage and living standard convergence in particular.

The chapter starts with a discussion of what should be used to measure convergence. It will focus on factor prices – including real wages – rather than GDP per capita or GDP per worker. Factor prices are far more useful in accessing the sources of convergence than are GDP aggregates, and they are also a far more relevant influence on policy. The chapter then summarizes the experience of the Atlantic economy with convergence between 1850 and 1914, contrasting it with the divergence between 1914 and 1950. The second chapter argues that it was open economy forces that were doing most of the work driving convergence prior to 1914 and divergence up to 1940. The third chapter sets the record straight on just who the gainers and losers were from these globalization forces. It documents income distribution trends around the Atlantic economy, a systematic rise in the rich, labor-scarce economies and a systematic decline in the poor, labor-abundant economies. This last lecture then explores the policy backlash to these globalization events. It starts with immigration policy responses in the labor-scarce New World, since it was mass migration which was doing most of the work driving convergence, and analysts of that time also thought it was mass migration doing most of the work creating inequality. Unskilled workers' absolute living standard experience and its behavior relative to that of the average citizen appear to have been the central ingredients of rising immigration restriction. Next, the lecture explores tariff responses in land-scarce Europe to the invasion of foodstuffs from the New World. The impact of these globalizing price shocks on land rents and landowners' wealth appear to have been the central ingredients of rising tariffs. I conclude these lectures with some remarks about whether this globalization backlash in our past is likely to reappear in our future.

1.2 Convergence in the present

Since the academic literature on the topic has become so plentiful, and since the issue even gets abundant media exposure, it is hard to imagine any intelligent citizen, and certainly any economist, who is unaware of the dramatic convergence which the Atlantic economy has undergone since 1950. By the Atlantic economy, I mean those which experienced industrialization first and who are now members of the OECD. These include North America, Australasia, and perhaps even the Latin American southern cone. By convergence, I mean the process by which poorer countries grew faster than richer countries in the Atlantic economy, the process by which the economic distance between them was eroded such that most of it eventually disappeared.

What explains this late twentieth-century convergence? Theoretical work is certainly plentiful, but it has usually been couched in terms of closed economies, theory which I think is more relevant for the decades between 1914 and 1970, rather than in terms of open economies, theory which I feel is more relevant for the decades since 1970. First generation growth models allowed for only unconditional convergence (Solow 1956), and thus were unable to deal with its frequent absence in the real world. Second generation models qualified or conditioned their growth predictions: divergence became possible by exploiting increasing returns, learning-by-doing, externalities, schooling, education, and skills (Romer 1986, 1989; Lucas 1988, 1990; Mankiw, Romer, and Weil 1992; Barro and Sala-i-Martin 1992, 1995). These "conditional" growth models have been much more successful in explaining the real world.

Empirical research on late twentieth-century convergence has come on in a rush. All of it has relied heavily on the post-World War II International Comparisons Project (ICP) data gathered in the series of Penn World Table publications (e.g., Summers and Heston 1991). Early on, economists found that as the sample expanded from the OECD to the rest of the world, conditional convergence became more apparent than unconditional convergence. Strong catch-up forces were at work everywhere, but many poor countries in the Third World only exhibited catching up when the researcher controlled for the fact that they were hampered by high population growth, low public savings rates, and human capital shortfalls (Barro 1991; Durlauf and Johnson 1992; Barro and Sala-i-Martin 1992; Mankiw, Romer, and Weil 1992). Thus, conditional controls are important if truly comprehensive convergence is to be uncovered even today.

Empirical applications of these conditional convergence models have advanced to such sophistication that they have been able to isolate the roles of openness, regulation, property rights, demography, natural resources, and even democracy (Barro 1996; Sachs and Warner 1995a, 1995b; Bloom and Williamson 1997; Williamson 1997b). For the most part, however, these models have been applied only to a tiny portion of history, the years since 1970. What about the vast stretch of history before?

Although less formal, historical work has also proliferated, led by the pioneering contributions of Moses Abramovitz (1986) and William Baumol (1986), each building on the long-run macroeconomic data collected by Angus Maddison (1982, 1989, 1991, 1995). Abramovitz related the observed catching up of post-war Europe on the United States to Veblen's "leader handicap" theory and Gerschenkron's "advantages of backwardness" theory: namely, a country with lower productivity can exploit the technological gap with respect to the leader, import or imitate best practice technology, and, hence, raise labor productivity and living standards. The leader has no gap to exploit, its productivity increases are limited by the rate at which new technology is applied to production, and so its growth is slower. The more backward the country, the bigger the technological gap, and the faster the potential catch-up or convergence. Abramovitz found gross domestic product (GDP) per worker dispersion to have diminished over the last century or so, although convergence was particularly rapid in the post-World War II period.

Abramovitz noted the distinction between convergence and technological catch-up since capital-deepening forces make it possible for the latter to be neither a necessary nor a sufficient condition for the former. Furthermore, he noted that technological catch-up would be self-limiting since it would decline to zero as the productivity gap diminished. Abramovitz also contrasted convergence measured by dispersion levels, now called σ-convergence, with convergence measured by the extent to which poor countries grow faster than rich, now called β-convergence (Barro and Sala-i-Martin 1992, 1995).

1.3 Is convergence a recent phenomenon?

Most economists take an a-historical position when writing about convergence in the late twentieth century. So it is that Robert Barro, Gregory Mankiw, and their collaborators (Barro and Sala-i-Martin 1992, 1995; Mankiw, Romer, and Weil 1992) ignore pre-World War II or even pre-1970 experience, focusing instead on the last two or three decades. The implicit assumption seems to be that the data for this kind of analysis are absent prior to the 1960s, or that the experience was irrelevant, or, even worse, that there could not possibly have been any convergence in pre-World War II history. Some even make the explicit assumption that it was only with the emergence of global institutions after Bretton Woods that convergence was possible, although even that historic 1944 accord was hostile to globally open capital markets. The few economists who look at a longer sweep of history often ignore the rich historical information embedded in their time series: William Baumol (1986) explored convergence over the century following 1870, but even this pioneer ignored all the decades in between (an oversight partially repaired in Baumol *et al.* 1989). And when Barro and Sala-i-Martin (1992) look at convergence between North American states since 1870, they too ignore the remarkable variance in convergence performance: there was none up to the 1930s; all the convergence occurred thereafter. Furthermore, it is rare for any economist looking at the experience since 1970 to ask how much of a region's or a country's growth performance is explained by the right-hand side variables. Instead, economists looking at the modern evidence use it solely for hypothesis testing: e.g., was there conditional catch-up, and was it faster under open economy policies? Historians demand more. They are always looking for deviant behavior, and then searching for explanations for it: e.g., which countries did not catch up when and why, and did all countries catching up do so for the same reason?

How great is the historical variety in convergence experience? Were the post-World War II years as unique as contemporary economists seem to imply? Or were the interwar years a profound interruption to a secular convergence started in the previous century? If the latter turns out to be the case, why the go, stop, go? And is there reason to expect another stop in the near future?

1.4 Convergence of what?

If I intend to show that history has a great deal to say about convergence, I must first define what I mean by the phrase. So, convergence of what?

The critical bottom line for me is whether the gap between the average worker's living standard in rich and poor countries falls over time. Convergence implies an erosion in this gap, at least in percentage terms. There appear to be two data sets that can be used to explore the issue over long time periods. GDP per worker-hour estimates offer one: Angus Maddison's data were originally published in 1982, superseded by his 1991 book, and now by even more recent revisions (Maddison 1994, 1995). Real wages offer another (Williamson 1995; recently revised in O'Rourke and Williamson 1997b).

Abramovitz, Baumol, and economists writing about the late twentieth century all use GDP per capita or per worker-hour to measure convergence. This lecture favors instead purchasing power parity adjusted real wage rates (typically urban unskilled). Real wages are certainly the right measure if our interest is the impact of globalization on labor markets. I am not suggesting that real wage or living standard data are necessarily superior to GDP per capita or GDP per worker-hour data for all questions involving the growth of nations. But I can think of four good reasons why we should look at factor prices – something which I will do throughout these chapters – in addition to GDP aggregates – which is all that macroeconomists look at when assessing the growth of nations.

First, the pre-World War I real wage data are possibly of better quality than the GDP data. They are available annually, rather than only for benchmark years separated by a couple of decades. And they are available for a wider sample of countries. Of course, it may be that the nominal wage series chosen is not representative, and there may be problems with the consumer price indices used to deflate, as well as with the PPP adjustments made. But these problems are surely smaller than those involved in trying to estimate nineteenth-century national incomes. For several countries around the European periphery (e.g., Ireland) nineteenth-century national accounts are simply unavailable, while existing series for others may well be unreliable.[1] At the very least, using real wages allows us to expand our sample of countries, reducing the risk of sample-selection bias identified by DeLong (1988) and others.

Second, income distribution matters. Real people earn unskilled wages, or skill premia, or profits, or land rents, not that statistical artifact known as GDP per capita. While GDP per worker-hour may be the right measure of aggregate productivity, the living standards of ordinary workers are better indicators of the economic well-being of a society.[2] It is in principle possible to design a tax and transfer system which could redistribute income between citizens leaving all equally well off, but such a scheme is as yet merely of theoretical interest, and must have seemed wildly utopian to late nineteenth-century observers. In any case, macroeconomists are throwing away valuable information by averaging all incomes.

Third, economic change nearly always involves losers as well as winners, and this fact is crucial to the evolution of economic policy. Changes that might increase GDP per capita are often

---

[1] Indeed, with each new revision of Maddison's GDP per capita estimates, inferences about pre-1940 convergence change (Williamson 1997b).

[2] Of course such a statement involves a value judgment, but so does the decision to focus on average incomes alone.

successfully resisted, and examining the behavior of factor prices is a necessary first step to understanding such political responses. Indeed, this is exactly the direction taken in my third chapter.

Fourth, and possibly most importantly, focusing on wages and other factor prices helps us understand the sources of convergence. The open economy mechanisms which I will argue were central in driving late nineteenth-century convergence – trade, migration, and capital flows – operated directly on factor prices, and thus only indirectly on GDP per capita. By focusing only on GDP per capita, macroeconomists are likely to miss a large part of the story. They may even make inferences that are just plain wrong. Suppose, for example, that we want to know whether convergence is due to technological catch-up, globalization through trade, or globalization through mass migration. If the dominant force is technological catch-up, then it seems likely that wage rates, land rents, and profit rates will all rise with GDP per capita and GDP per worker, albeit at different rates depending on some technological bias (Aghion 1997). If the dominant force is globalization through trade, then the standard Heckscher–Ohlin trade theory discussed in the next lecture predicts that wage–rental ratios will move in opposite directions in the two trading partners, and that factor prices will converge much faster than either GDP per capita or GDP per worker. If the dominant force is mass migration, and if, as was the case, the migrants tended to be young adults, then in immigrant countries GDP per capita should rise faster than GDP per worker, and wage rates should fall relative to land rents and profit rates. The opposite would be true of emigrant countries. By relying solely on GDP per worker or GDP per capita data, macroeconomists are missing a chance to discriminate between these and other competing explanations for convergence.

1.5   Divergence shocks and convergence responses, 1830–1870

The Atlantic economy was perturbed by two profound shocks in the first half of the nineteenth century: early industrialization in Britain which then spread to a few countries on the European

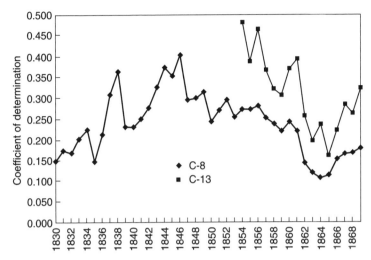

Figure 1.1 International real wage dispersion, 1830–1869
Source: O'Rourke and Williamson (1997a, figure 1.1).

continent; and resource "discovery" in the New World, triggered
by sharply declining international transport costs which raised
the prices of those resources at the frontier to lofty heights. Tariff
barriers were high prior to mid century even in Britain (the Corn
Laws were repealed only in 1846, with liberal trade reform following on the European continent a decade or two thereafter); commodity trade was modest; migration across national borders was
not yet "mass" (the famine-induced Irish flood of migrants was
not released until the late 1840s); and capital markets were as yet
underdeveloped and not quite global. The divergence can only be
documented starting 1830, and even then the sample is relatively
small (eight countries in 1830, rising to thirteen by 1869).
Nonetheless, the limited evidence points to steep divergence
during the first half of the century.

Figure 1.1 documents real wage dispersion between 1830 and
1869. The summary statistic $C(N)$ plotted there (where N is the
sample size) has been used extensively in the convergence debate,
and it is my measure of σ-convergence.[3] Based on the eight Atlantic

---

[3] The statistic C is defined as a variance divided by the square of the mean, equivalent to the coefficient of variation, but easier to decompose.

countries for which data are available (Brazil, France, Great Britain, Ireland, The Netherlands, Spain, Sweden, and the United States), $C(8)$ rises from 0.143 in 1830 to 0.402 in 1846, a near-tripling in the index of real wage and living standard dispersion over the three decades. This global labor-market disequilibrium was driven primarily by a wage boom in the United States and a wage slump in Spain and The Netherlands (Williamson 1995, appendix table A2.1; revised in O'Rourke and Williamson 1997b). Relative to the European leader of the pack (Britain), Ireland and France held their own while Sweden lost some ground. Industrial revolutionary events in Europe certainly contributed to this divergence phase up to the mid 1840s, but the sharp rise in $C(8)$ is due primarily to New World success: the United States increased her real wage advantage over England from 45 percent in 1830 to 89 percent in 1846.[4] This is a surprising finding given that the British standard of living debate points to wage improvement during these decades as unambiguous support for the optimists' position (Lindert and Williamson 1983; Lindert 1994). Apparently, real wage gains in Britain were far less significant than they were in America. The British standard of living debate has never noticed this fact, nor, for that matter, have the American "exceptionalists" made very much of the impressive US relative wage performance.

While we do not have similar real wage data this early in the century for, say, Canada or Australia, the American evidence certainly suggests that the global labor-market disequilibrium was being driven primarily by rising wage gaps between Europe and the English-speaking New World. Does it follow that there were no Gerschenkron-like industrial-leader and latecomer–follower dynamics which augmented wage gaps in Europe? No. We must remember an inherent selectivity bias underlying this small sample of six European economies: it excludes many poorly documented latecomers. The dispersion within Europe is likely to have risen far more than these figures suggest. Thus, the sharp divergence in the Atlantic economy measured here understates the true magnitude of that event.

---

[4] While per capita incomes were still quite a bit higher in England, real wages were quite a different matter.

Figure 1.1 suggests a secular turning point somewhere between 1846 – based on the smaller but longer sample underlying $C(8)$ – and 1854 – based on the larger but shorter sample underlying $C(13)$. Since convergence persists for the next six decades or so, the mid nineteenth century appears to date the start of modern convergence in the Atlantic economy. True, a good share of the real wage convergence between 1854 and 1865 can be explained by the well-known collapse of American wages during the Civil War, but this early convergence was more general than this exogenous and country-specific event would imply. After all, the otherwise impressive American post-bellum real wage recovery in the late 1860s and 1870s never led to the high wages relative to Britain achieved at the peak in 1854–1856 (105 percent). Furthermore, relative wages also fell in Australia after 1854, suggesting it was an event common to more of the New World than simply North America. The results were mixed in Europe. While Sweden gained a lot of ground on Britain between the mid 1850s and 1869, none of the other European countries in our Atlantic sample did (with the possible exception of Belgium), and France, Norway, and Spain actually lost ground. Once again, it appears that the convergence from mid century to 1869 was driven primarily by the erosion of the gap between Europe and the New World.

Three morals have emerged from our look at Atlantic labor markets over the four decades between 1830 and 1869. First, there was a very sharp divergence in real wages and living standards up to mid century. Second, convergence in the Atlantic economy started shortly after mid century. True, the Atlantic sample is still small around mid century, but it rises to seventeen by 1870 (including five New World countries) so we should be more certain about convergence trends starting then. This date is commonly used by economic historians in describing other events anyway, and the "late nineteenth century" typically refers to the years starting 1870 and ending with World War I. Third, divergence and convergence were both driven by the behavior of wage gaps between Europe and the New World, as well as by the behavior of wage gaps within Europe.

1.6 Late nineteenth-century convergence

Economists are taught that really important shocks to any market are followed, with a lag, by the transition to a new equilibria or a new steady state, unless, of course, it is arrested by state intervention. One might view late nineteenth-century convergence as one such transition in globally integrating commodity, labor, and capital markets around the Atlantic economy, one in which the state took a liberal view of the transition.

The Argentineans call the transition from 1870 to 1913 the "belle époque," North Americans refer to it as their "gilded age" of industrial take off to world dominance, the English dub it their "great Victorian boom" carried on a wave of high imperialism, but most economists are taught to view it as a liberal era of free trade under the gold standard.[5] If the two decades prior to 1870 are included, it was the most extensive real wage and living standard convergence the Atlantic economy has seen since 1830, including the better-known convergence of the post-World War II era. However, most of the convergence was completed by the turn of the century, and the "speed" per decade was not as fast as that recorded during the post-World War II epoch (Crafts and Toniolo 1996), but it was an impressive convergence nonetheless.

As figure 1.2 shows, the striking convergence which started in mid century continued up to around 1900, after which the decline in $C(17)$ ceased.[6] In fact, it drops by more than a third over the three decades 1870–1900 (falling from 0.313 to 0.200), and drops perhaps by two thirds over the half century following 1854. Our summary measure of real wage differences across countries, C, can be decomposed into three additive parts: dispersion within the New World; dispersion within Europe; and dispersion between Europe and the New World, the latter measured by the average wage gap between the two. When these three components are computed, the results are striking, and repeat a message found earlier in the century (Williamson 1996). First, throughout the period 1870–1913, the average wage gap between Europe and

---

[5] Maddison (1982: p. 92) calls it the "liberal" phase.
[6] The time series in figure 1.2 labeled I-13 and N-15 will be discussed below.

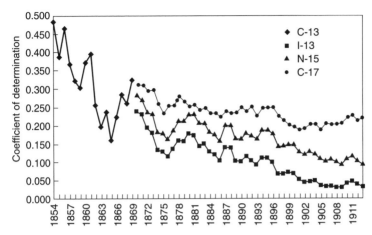

Figure 1.2 International real wage dispersion, 1854–1913
Source: O'Rourke and Williamson (1997a, figure 1.2).

the New World accounts for about 60 percent of the real wage variance across these seventeen countries. The remainder, 40 percent, is explained by the variance within Europe and the New World. Furthermore, real wage variance within the New World accounts for more of the total variance than does real wage variance within Europe. All of this implies that real wage variance among our late nineteenth-century European countries was a very modest part of real wage variance in the Atlantic economy as a whole (although I have already confessed that the absence of poor East European nations from the sample probably accounts for much of this result). Second, about 60 percent of the convergence between 1870 and 1900 is explained by the collapse in the wage gap between Europe and the New World.

Late nineteenth-century convergence was not limited to real wages and labor markets. Figure 1.3 shows that GDP per capita converged as well. However, real wage convergence was a lot faster than GDP per capita or GDP per worker-hour convergence, and the globalization arguments which follow offer some reasons why.

Convergence was ubiquitous in the late nineteenth-century Atlantic economy, but it was mostly a story about labor abundant Europe with the lower workers' living standards catching up with the labor scarce New World with the higher workers' living

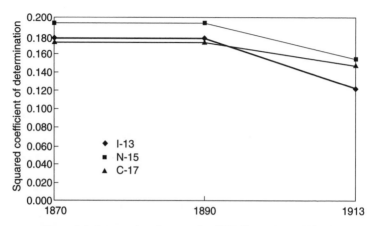

Figure 1.3 International per capita GDP dispersion, 1870–1913
Source: Maddison (1995).

standards, and of Argentina and Canada catching up with Australia and the United States. It was less a story about European industrial latecomers catching up with European industrial leaders. Convergence did take place within Europe, but it was a modest affair in the aggregate since spectacular catching-up successes on the continent were offset by some equally spectacular failures. This European experience deserves a closer look.

Given the great debate about Britain's loss of industrial leadership, there is a tendency to look for evidence of, say, German catch-up on the leader. In spite of the enormous outpouring of literature on Britain's loss of leadership to America and Germany, it is definitely the wrong place to look if the purpose is to understand European convergence or lack of it. Germany was certainly not one of the poorer countries in the Atlantic economy, and America even less so. The switch in roles between these big three – Britain, Germany, and the United States – involved an exchange of leadership among the leaders, an interesting event, but marginal to the issue at hand. What mattered far more was the behavior of the poorer agricultural European countries relative to the richer industrial ones, and the richer included Belgium, France, and Germany, not just Britain.

Before I proceed with the narrative, let me first define the European sample. Table 1.1 reports 1870 real wages and GDP per

Table 1.1. *Who is in the European periphery sample?*

Country	(1) Real wage per urban worker, 1870 (GB 1905 = 100)		(2) Real GDP per head 1870 (1990 US$)	
The European periphery				
Austria	na	(na)	1847	(101)
Denmark	36	(85)	1836	(101)
Finland	na	(na)	1095	(60)
Ireland	49	(115)	na	(na)
Italy	26	(61)	1568	(86)
Norway	32	(75)	1229	67)
Portugal	18	(42)	793	(43)
Spain	30	(70)	1338	(76)
Sweden	28	(66)	1596	(87)
Average	**31**	**(73)**	**1419**	**(78)**
The European industrial core				
Belgium	60	(141)	2572	(141)
France	50	(117)	1935	(106)
Germany	58	(136)	1619	(89)
Great Britain	67	(157)	3115	(171)
The Netherlands	57	(134)	2490	(136)
Switzerland	na	(na)	2476	(136)
Average	**58**	**(137)**	**2368**	**(130)**
Europe	**43**	**(100)**	**1826**	**(100)**

Source: O'Rourke and Williamson (1997a: table 1).

head for fifteen European countries. The two indices reveal similar rankings, but they imply different gaps between these countries: as predicted, there were bigger gaps between real wages than between GDP per capita and GDP per worker aggregates. The rich industrial core countries had levels of GDP per head 67 percent higher than the poor agricultural periphery. Their real wages were 86 percent higher than the periphery. Alternatively, real wages in the periphery were 46 percent below the industrial core average and GDP per head was 40 percent below. Austria and Denmark seem to have been on the margin between core and periphery: without them, the periphery GDP per head would have been 46 percent below the industrial core average, not 40 percent below. Nonetheless, I throw Austria and Denmark in with the periphery countries. Thus, the nine members of the European periphery are: Austria, Denmark, Finland, Ireland, Italy, Norway, Portugal, Spain, and Sweden. Note again that the sample excludes east and southeast Europe simply because the historical data are inadequate for those regions. Still, they were, of course, relatively poor. Paul Bairoch's (1976: table 6, p. 286) guestimates suggest that none of them had levels of GDP per head that were even half that of the core: e.g., Bulgaria, 42.3 percent of the core; Greece, 48.1 percent; Romania, 40.4 percent; Russia, 48.1 percent; and Serbia, 44.2 percent. Thus, with the exception of Portugal, these chapters ignore the poorest part of Europe. Hopefully, as better historical data emerge from east and southeast Europe they will confirm the assertions which follow.

Let me start with the success in the north, the spectacular Scandinavian catch up on the leaders. Consistent with qualitative accounts, the evidence in table 1.2 confirms that Sweden and Denmark tended to outperform Norway and Finland, but not by much. While real wages show Sweden growing considerably faster than Norway, GDP per capita growth and GDP per worker-hour growth reveal only modest differences between the two fastest and the two slowest. Rapid growth seems to have been common to all four Nordic countries.

Real wages in Scandinavia grew at rates almost three times those prevailing in the European industrial core; Swedish workers enjoyed real wage growth about 2.7 times that of British workers; Danish workers enjoyed real wage growth about 2.6 times that of German workers; and Norwegian workers enjoyed real wage growth about 3.8 times that of Dutch workers. In fact, no other country in our European sample underwent real wage growth even close to that of Sweden, Denmark, or Norway.

Table 1.2 also documents trends in the wage–rental ratio. It tells us how the unskilled worker's wage behaved relative to farm rents or farm land values per acre. While not an indicator of performance per se, such relative factor price movements will be an important

Table 1.2. *Relative economic performance of the European periphery in the late nineteenth century: growth per annum (%)*

	(1) Real wage per urban worker 1870–1913	(2) Wage–rental ratio 1879–1910	(3) Real GDP per capita 1870–1913	(4) Real GDP per worker hour 1870–1913
The European periphery				
Denmark	2.63	2.85	1.57	1.90
Finland	na	na	1.44	1.80
Norway	2.43	na	1.31	1.65
Sweden	2.73	2.45	1.46	1.74
Scandinavia	2.60	2.65	1.45	1.77
Italy	1.74	na	1.28	1.33
Portugal	0.37	na	0.69	1.10
Spain	0.44	− 0.43	1.11	1.52
Mediterranean Basin				
with Italy	0.85	− 0.43	1.03	1.32
without Italy	0.41	− 0.43	0.90	1.31
Austria	na	na	1.46	1.76
Ireland	1.79	4.39	na	na
Other Periphery	1.79	4.39	1.46	1.76
Periphery	**1.73**	**2.32**	**1.29**	**1.60**
The European Industrial Core				
Belgium	0.92	na	1.05	1.24
France	0.91	1.80	1.30	1.58
Germany	1.02	0.87	1.63	1.88
Great Britain	1.03	2.54	1.01	1.23
The Netherlands	0.64	na	1.01	1.34
Switzerland	na	na	1.20	1.46
Industrial Core	0.90	1.74	1.20	1.46
Europe	1.39	2.10	1.25	1.54
The New World				
Argentina	1.74	− 4.06	na	na
Australia	0.14	− 3.30	0.87	1.08
Canada	1.65	na	2.29	2.31
USA	1.04	− 1.72	1.81	1.93
New World	**1.14**	**− 3.03**	**1.66**	**1.77**

Notes: All averages are unweighted.
Source: O'Rourke and Williamson (1997a: table 2).

analytical component of the open economy hypotheses I will be exploring. While the ratio of wage rates per worker to farm land values per acre fell everywhere in the New World, it rose everywhere in Europe (with the exception of Spain). These events reflect the invasion of grains from the New World (and Russia) which lowered farm rents and land values in Europe and raised them in the American Midwest, the Australian outback, the Argentine pampas, and, I assume but do not document, the Ukraine. While the Scandinavian wage–rental ratio seems to have tracked the British ratio very closely (2.65 versus 2.54 percent per annum growth), the ratio rose half again faster in Scandinavia than in the European industrial core (2.65 versus 1.74 percent per annum).

Consistent with the predictions of conventional trade theory, product per worker-hour documents a less spectacular Scandinavian catch-up than do factor prices, but even these data confirm an impressive growth performance compared with the European industrial core (1.77 versus 1.46 percent per annum). Consistent with the fact that Scandinavian emigrants were economically active, the superiority of Scandinavian GDP per capita growth over that of the industrial core (1.45 versus 1.2 percent per annum) is smaller than that of GDP per worker-hour, but it is still superior.

Scandinavia outperformed the rest of Europe (and probably the rest of the world) in the late nineteenth century, of that there can be no doubt. They were over-achievers even by catching-up standards.[7] What about the rest of the periphery?

Based on Maddison's data, Austria seems to have done about as well as Scandinavia: GDP per capita and GDP per worker-hour grew almost exactly as fast (1.46 versus 1.45 and 1.76 versus 1.77). In contrast, while Ireland certainly obeyed the laws of convergence, it was no over-achiever. Irish real wages grew twice as fast as they did in the industrial core (1.79 versus 0.90 per annum), but they grew about as fast as the periphery average, and they recorded only three-quarters of the Scandinavia growth rate. On the other hand, the Irish wage–rental ratio rose faster.

---

[7] All of these assertions here and in the next paragraph have been successfully tested with conditional convergence models (O'Rourke and Williamson (1997a: chapter 1; 1997b)).

The western Mediterranean Basin did very badly. The Iberian peninsula fell far behind the growth rates recorded in the rest of the periphery. Real wages crawled upwards at about 0.4 percent a year in Iberia, while they surged five and a half times as quickly elsewhere around the periphery. Like so many Third World countries during the second great globalization boom over the past quarter century, Spain and Portugal seem to have missed out on the first great globalization boom – as did Egypt, Turkey, and Serbia at the other end of the Mediterranean Basin. While the wage–rental ratio soared at 3.23 percent a year elsewhere around the periphery, it fell by 0.43 percent a year in Iberia. The same wide gap appears for GDP per capita growth, 0.9 percent per annum in Iberia and 1.42 percent per annum elsewhere around the periphery. Maddison's real GDP per worker-hour data also confirm a poor Iberian performance, but the gap is not quite so great, as open economy arguments would predict: 1.31 percent per annum in Iberia (slower than in the core, confirming Iberian "fall-back") and 1.7 percent per annum around the rest of the periphery. Italy does somewhat better, but even she – except for real wages – falls below the average for the periphery. The importance of the Iberian failure to overall Atlantic economy convergence has already been seen in figure 1.2: the convergence from 1854 to 1913 is steeper when the Iberians are removed (I-13 versus N-15).

Let me now return to the average wage gap between Europe and the New World, the variable which accounted for so much of the convergence over the half century. Four countries illustrate the process best, Ireland and Sweden (with heavy emigrations from the late 1840s onwards); the United States (with heavy immigrations from the late 1840s onwards); and Britain (the industrial leader, losing its dominant grip). In 1856, unskilled real wages in urban Sweden were only 49 percent of Britain, while in 1913 they were at parity, an impressive doubling in Sweden's wage relative over the fifty-seven years. Sweden's real wages rose from 24 percent to 58 percent of the United States over the same period. In 1852, and shortly after the famine, unskilled real wages in urban Ireland were only 61 percent of Britain, a figure that had changed hardly at all over the previous three decades. Real wages in Ireland started a dramatic convergence on Britain during the 1850s (and, notably, in the absence of any Irish industrialization) so that they were 73 percent of Britain by 1870. They were 92 percent of Britain by 1913. Ireland was transformed over this period of convergence from a desperately poor, poverty-stricken, peasant economy which had served as a source of cheap labor for booming cities in Britain and North America, to an economy at the start of the twentieth century which boasted wages close to those prevailing across the Irish Sea (and which came to exceed British wages in the 1920s). Irish convergence on the booming US economy was less dramatic, but convergence there was: Irish real wages increased from 43 to 53 percent of US real wages between 1855 and 1913.

These patterns were sufficiently ubiquitous to have produced real wage and standard of living convergence in the Atlantic economy over the half century or more prior to World War I. But, as I have already suggested, there were some deviant countries and periods which failed to conform to secular convergence patterns. It might be useful to cite them again.

First, the experience in the English-speaking New World varied. Australia experienced a steady erosion in her real wage position over the whole period of convergence – from 148 to 90 percent above the British real wage between 1854 and 1870, to 47 percent above in 1890 and to just 31 percent above in 1913. But the other New World countries enjoyed a partial resurrection in their real wage advantage late in the regime. This was especially true of North America. Relative to Britain, real wages in the United States were 106 percent higher in 1855, 72 percent higher in 1870, 44 percent higher in 1880, but 72 percent higher in 1913 (after a great industrialization boom which pushed America into world leadership). Real wages in Canada were 48 percent higher than in Britain in 1870, 55 percent higher in 1880, but 123 percent higher in 1913 (after the great wheat boom and railroad expansion of which so much is made by Canadian economic historians). In short, both Canada and the United States buck the convergence tide after the mid 1890s. This result is consistent with North America's emerging industrial dominance about that time (Wright 1990), and it makes America's successful defence of her economic leadership for so long thereafter all the more impressive. North America's stubborn unwillingness to allow others to catch-up matters to overall measures of convergence in the Atlantic economy. The σ-convergence from 1854 to 1913 in Figure 1.2 is much greater when the North American experience is removed (the series labeled N-15 versus C-17).

Second, the Latin experience was very different on both sides of the Atlantic. We have already seen that Iberia fell further behind the core during the late nineteenth century. Namely, when both the poor performance of Portugal and Spain and the good performance of Canada and the United States are removed, convergence is faster (the series I-13 in figure 1.2) compared with that when just the two North American countries are removed (the series N-15 in figure 1.2). Meanwhile, through dramatic booms and busts, Argentina increased her real wage advantage over Spain and Italy, the source of the vast majority of her immigrants. Argentina improved her real wage position even relative to Britain, from 76 percent in 1864 to 94 percent in 1913, and her real wages actually exceeded Britain in 1888, 1893, 1899, 1900, 1904, and 1912 (an achievement that Argentineans view today with nostalgia). Thus, Argentina, and, presumably, her neighbors Chile and Uruguay, offer a Latin exception to the more general rule that European wages were catching up with the New World in the late nineteenth century: the low-wage Southern Cone was catching up to high-wage Britain.

1.7 What a difference factor prices make

What do we make of the fact that the two most prominent contributors to the historical convergence literature, Moses Abramovitz and William Baumol, make so little of these nineteenth-century convergence forces which seem to be so pronounced in the real wage data used here? In Abramovitz's words: "the rate of convergence ... showed marked strength only during the first quarter-century following World War II"; and "in the years of relative peace before 1913 ... the process [of convergence] left a weak mark on the record" (1986: pp. 385 and 395). Of course,

Abramovitz and Baumol looked at GDP per capita or GDP per worker-hour, while this lecture uses purchasing-power-parity adjusted real wage rates. We have already seen how the convergence behavior of these three measures differed in the past, real wages and other factor prices converging far faster than the GDP aggregates. Now consider three reasons why this was so.

First, GDP per worker is nothing more than a sum of per unit factor returns weighted by factor endowments per worker. Factor price convergence does not imply that all factor prices in the rich country fall relative to the poor. Some rise. Suppose the initially rich countries are land abundant and labor scarce, while the initially poor countries are land scarce and labor abundant. While factor price convergence implies that low wages in poor countries catch up to high wages in rich countries, it also implies that low land rents in rich countries catch up to high land rents in poor countries. A similar argument applies to the premium on skills and schooling. Thus, theory suggests that wage convergence is likely to be more dramatic than GDP per worker convergence, and that relative factor price convergence (e.g., the wage–rental ratio) is likely to be most dramatic. The historical facts from the globalization boom prior to World War I seem to be consistent with theory.

Second, the deflators for GDP and wage rates will always differ. In a world of very incomplete commodity price equalization, the difference may matter, especially since laborers heavily consume wage goods which are expensive to move internationally (e.g., dwelling space and foodstuffs are a very big share of their total expenditures), more heavily than do white-collar employees, big landowners, and successful capitalists. The truth of this statement is easy to defend for the previous century when declining transport costs edged the global economy closer to commodity price equalization, especially in the grain market, but also for butter, cheese, and meats. The commodity price gaps between countries that eroded most were foodstuffs, not finished manufactures. Thus, the worker's cost of living converged more dramatically across labor markets than did the GDP implicit price deflator, helping real wages converge faster than GDP per worker and, hence, faster than labor productivity.

Third, the labor participation rate can differ greatly between countries and over time in an environment of migration and differential rates of population growth, driving a wedge between per capita and per worker indices. If the forces of early demographic transition (declining infant mortality, but persistent high fertility) are strongest for richer countries, causing population growth to exceed labor force growth by more in richer countries, then per capita convergence will be faster than per worker convergence. If the forces of mass migration dominate instead, then the opposite will be true since migrants were disproportionately young adult males. That is, if mass migration dominates, it will serve to raise labor participation rates in rich immigrating countries and lower them in poor emigrating countries, causing per capita convergence to be slower than per worker convergence.

Do any of these considerations imply that the real wage data overstate convergence? Absolutely, but it is equally true that the GDP per worker data understate convergence. Factor prices, average productivity, and per capita income should exhibit different convergence properties. I rely on factor prices since they matter far more in effecting the policy responses discussed at the end of these chapters.

1.8 Adding the rest of the world

At the beginning of this chapter, I reported that the literature on recent convergence makes much of the fact that, while unconditional convergence has taken place in the Atlantic economy since the 1950s, conditional growth models are required when the convergence net is extended to capture the Third World. The same is true of the nineteenth century: European unconditional convergence prior to 1914 was limited mainly to the Atlantic economy as I have defined it. Using Bairoch's guestimates (1976: table 6), there is absolutely no evidence of convergence when central, south, and east European countries like Austria-Hungary, Bulgaria, Greece, and Russia are added. The point could be made even more forcefully if China, Egypt, India, Turkey, and the rest of Asia, and the Middle East were added to the analysis.

This chapter has a more limited goal: to account for the sources of convergence within the Atlantic economy. I leave the additional (and perhaps tougher) question about when and why new members joined the convergence club for another time.

1.9   The collapse of convergence under autarky 1914–1950

North America's leap to industrial dominance after the 1890s would, by itself, have slowed down convergence in the Atlantic economy. Already relatively rich due to abundant resources and scarce labor, it got even richer due to industrialization. But secular convergence stopped for other reasons too.

Between 1914 and 1934, real wage dispersion did not fall at all, implying that the secular convergence which had been at work since the middle of the nineteenth century stopped completely during these two decades. Following 1934, real wage gaps in the Atlantic economy widened so much that measures of global labor-market (dis)integration retreated all the way back to the levels of the late 1870s.

The World Wars and the interwar decades offer nothing but contrast to the secular convergence of real wages and living standards initiated in the mid nineteenth-century Atlantic economy. As figure 1.4 confirms, the convergence ceases between 1914 and 1937. The cessation of real wage convergence documented here offers a very different characterization than that reported by *Productivity and American Leadership*. When Baumol and his associates plot the coefficient of variation beyond 1913 and up to the mid 1930s (based on Maddison's GDP data), convergence continues its long-run decline initiated in 1870.[8] Indeed, they state that convergence "has proceeded steadily, with the exception of a brief but sharp fallback during and after World War II" (Baumol *et al.* 1989: p. 92). The real wage data suggest the contrary: secular convergence ceased between 1914 and 1937. And figure 1.5 shows that Maddison's revised GDP per capita data

[8] Abramovitz (1986: table 1, p. 391) found the same.

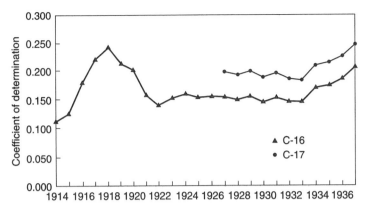

Figure 1.4 International real wage dispersion, 1914–1937
Source: Williamson (1995, table A2.1; revised in O'Rourke and
Williamson 1997b).

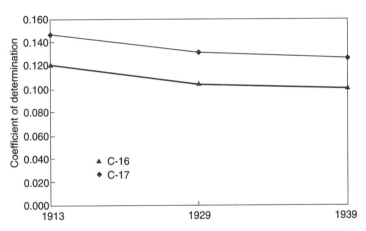

Figure 1.5 International per capita GDP dispersion, 1914–1937
Source: Maddison (1995).

(unavailable to Abramovitz or to Baumol and his collaborators)
also implies that secular convergence slowed down sharply after
1913 and pretty much stopped after 1929.

The interwar cessation of convergence could not have been
due to the Great Depression alone since there is no evidence of
real wage convergence during the 1920s either. Furthermore,

after World War I overall trends in real wage dispersion were dominated by wage events in Europe, not the average real wage gap between Europe and the New World that was so true of convergence prior to World War I.

Real wage divergence took place after 1934 and up through World War II and it took place everywhere – within Europe, within the New World, and between the two. A large share of that divergence was driven by the spectacular surge in real wages in the US,[9] but, to repeat, it was at work everywhere. The divergence during the dismal decade 1935–1945 was so spectacular that all of the convergence gains up to the start of World War I were lost by the end of World War II. Note, too, that divergence rose during the late 1930s at a rate almost as steep as during the war years. Since our real wage rates do not take account of unemployment, and since unemployment rates in the United States in 1934 were far higher than elsewhere, the surge in American unemployment-adjusted real wages from 1934 on would be even greater and the measured divergence greater as well.

How much of the war and interwar cessation of convergence can be explained by the breakdown of international commodity and factor markets?

The correlation is certainly apparent. After the passage of the Quota Acts in the 1920s, the United States would never again have an open immigration policy, and Argentina, Australia, Brazil, and Canada soon followed suit. International migrations between members of the Atlantic economy, and between non-members and members, dropped from a massive flood to a modest trickle, not to become a public issue again until the 1980s when non-members from Asia, Africa, and Latin America began to send emigrants (legal and illegal) in large numbers to the Atlantic economy. Governments intervened in capital markets, restricting the movements of financial capital across their borders. This hostility toward global capital markets was even manifested at Bretton Woods. The enormous flow of private capital from western Europe (led by Britain) to the Americas, to eastern Europe and to Europe's colonies dried up, not to recover until the

---

[9] See also Abramovitz (1986: p. 395) and Wolff (1991: p. 569).

1970s. Commodity trade was choked off by tariffs, quotas, preferential agreements, and exchange rate intervention, a protectionist shift that was to take decades of GATT, EC, NAFTA, and other negotiations to erase after World War II.

Is the correlation spurious? If I can show that convergence in the late nineteenth century was driven largely or even significantly by open economy forces in Atlantic commodity and factor markets, then it would invite the inference that the disintegration of the Atlantic economy between 1914 and 1950 had a great deal to do with the cessation of the secular convergence that started in the middle of the previous century.

1.10 Searching for causes and assessing the consequences

One way or another, the remaining two chapters speak to this issue. What form did global integration take from the mid nineteenth century to World War I? What exactly was its impact on labor markets in the Atlantic economy? Did contemporaries recognize the impact? Did these globalization events produce a policy backlash?

TWO

Globalization and the causes of workers' living standard convergence in the past

2.1 Why did wages and living standards converge?

The previous lecture established that wages and living standards in the Atlantic economy converged up to World War I. Convergence stopped thereafter, not starting again until 1950.

What caused the convergence, and why did it stop? Listing the possible causes is easy enough. The hard part is to identify which of them was most important. First, there is the possible impact of globalization in commodity markets: that is, the impact of trade itself when it surged in the six decades following mid century. Second, there is the possible impact of globalization in factor markets: that is, the impact of the mass migrations which reached a peak prior to World War I that never has been surpassed, and the impact of international capital flows which created a global capital market that was at least as well integrated as it is today. Third, there is the possible impact of technology transfer, the poor follower economies borrowing industrial, transport, and agricultural best-practice technologies from the rich leaders.

This essay draws heavily on my own previous work (Williamson 1996) and that with three collaborators: Alan Taylor (Taylor and Williamson 1997); Timothy J. Hatton (Hatton and Williamson 1997); and Kevin O'Rourke (O'Rourke and Williamson 1997a, 1997b). I gratefully acknowledge the collaboration with these three colleagues, and their generous permission to allow me to draw on our joint work for this lecture.

Finally, there are all the closed economy forces which figure so prominently in the new growth theory: compared with the rich, the successful poor countries exhibit more rapid skill formation, more rapid capital accumulation, and more rapid total factor productivity advance, all of which might contribute to catching up, and none of which need be related to globalization.

What does history tell us? Did globalization cause wage and living standard convergence in the Atlantic economy prior to 1914, or instead was it closed economy, catch-up forces at work?

2.2 The amazing decline in international transport costs

I use the term "amazing" in this sub-title advisedly because the decline in international transport costs after mid century was enormous, and it ushered in a new era. When economists look at this period, they tend to ignore this fact and focus instead on tariffs and trade. This is a mistake. The volume of trade itself is an unsatisfactory index of commodity market integration. It is the cost of moving goods between markets that counts. The cost has two parts, that due to transport and that due to trade barriers (such as tariffs). The price spread between markets is driven by changes in these costs. It turns out that tariffs in the Atlantic economy did not fall from the 1870s to World War I; the globalization which took place in the late nineteenth century cannot be assigned to more liberal trade policy. Instead, it was falling transport costs which provoked globalization. Indeed, rising tariffs were mainly a response to the competitive winds of market integration as transport costs declined.

Prior to the railway era, transportation was either by road or water, with water being the cheaper option by far. Investment in river and harbor improvements increased briskly, and the construction of canals overwhelmed the construction of turnpikes after the mid eighteenth century. British navigable waterways quadrupled between 1750 and 1820 and canals offered a transport option 50–75 percent cheaper than roads (Girard 1966: 223). French canal construction boomed. The completion of the Erie canal in 1825 reduced the cost of transport between Buffalo and New York by 85 percent, and the journey time was cut by almost two weeks, from 21 to 8 days.

Steamships were the most important nineteenth-century contribution to shipping technology. By 1816, a steamer had made the journey up the Mississippi as far as Louisville, and British steamers had travelled up the Seine. In the first half of the century, steamships were mainly used on important rivers, the Great Lakes, and inland seas like the Baltic and the Mediterranean. A regular trans-Atlantic steam service was inaugurated in 1838, but until 1860 steamers mainly carried high-value goods similar to those carried by airplanes today, like passengers, mail, and gourmet food. A series of innovations in subsequent decades helped make steamships more efficient: the screw propeller, the compound engine, steel hulls, bigger size, and shorter turn-around time. Equally important was the opening of the Suez Canal in 1869.

The other major nineteenth-century transportation development was the railroad. The Liverpool–Manchester line opened in 1830 and continental emulators included Belgium, France, and Germany. The railroad would play a major role in creating a truly national market in the United States. Indeed, the railroad was in many ways to the United States what the 1992 Single Market program was to the European Union. Alfred Chandler (1977) has shown how the single US market facilitated the creation of pan-American companies, foreshadowing the European merger wave of the 1990s. There was also a federal move to regulate firms and markets in the late nineteenth-century United States just as Brussels is today appropriating powers to regulate companies operating throughout the European Union, and for very similar reasons.

The impact of these productivity improvements on transport costs around the Atlantic economy can be seen graphically in figure 2.1. What is labeled the North index (North 1958) accelerates its fall after the 1830s, and what is labeled the British index (Harley 1988) is fairly stable up to mid century before undergoing the same, big fall. The North freight rate index among American export routes dropped by more than 41 percent in real terms

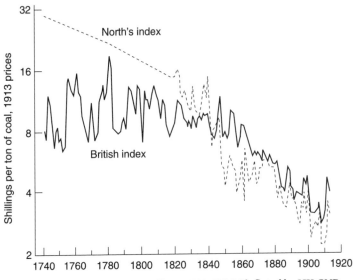

Figure 2.1 Freight rate indices, 1741–1913 (deflated by UK GNP deflator)
Source: Harley (1988, figure 1).

between 1870 and 1910. The British index fell by about 70 percent, again in real terms, between 1840 and 1910. These two indices imply a steady decline in Atlantic economy transport costs of about 1.5 percent per annum, for a total of 45 percentage points up to 1913, a big number indeed. There is another way to get a comparative feel for the magnitude of this decline. The World Bank reports that tariffs on manufactures entering developed country markets fell from 40 percent in the late 1940s to 7 percent in the late 1970s, a 33 percentage point decline over thirty years (Wood 1994: 173). While impressive, this spectacular post-war reclamation of "free trade" from interwar autarky is still smaller than the 45 percentage point fall in trade barriers between 1870 and 1913 due to transport improvements.

Transport costs are not everything. Transit time also fell, lowering inventory costs. Refrigeration was another technological innovation with major trade implications. Mechanical refrigeration was developed between 1834 and 1861, and by 1870 chilled beef was being transported from the United States to Europe. In

1876, the first refrigerated ship sailed from Argentina to France carrying frozen beef, and by the 1880s South American and Australian meat, and New Zealand butter, were being exported in large quantities to Europe (Mokyr 1990). Not only did railways and steamships mean that European farmers were faced with overseas competition in the grain market, but refrigeration also deprived them of the natural protection distance had always provided local meat and dairy producers. The consequences of this overseas competition for European farmers would be profound.

Transport costs between the American Midwest and East Coast fell even more dramatically than trans-Atlantic transport costs during the late nineteenth century. The British Board of Trade published in 1903 an annual series of transport costs for the wheat trade between Chicago, New York, and Liverpool. It cost 6s.11d. to ship a quarter of wheat by lake and rail from Chicago to New York in 1868. The cost using rail alone was 10s.2d. The cost of shipping a quarter of wheat from New York to Liverpool by steamer was 4s.7d. In 1902, these costs had fallen to 1s.11d., 2s.11d., and 0s.11d. respectively. The percentage decline in trans-Atlantic costs may have been greater, but in absolute terms it was the technical improvements on American railways that did most of the work in reducing price gaps between US producer and British consumer.

I could easily multiply these examples, but the ones offered should serve to motivate the central question. Did these rail and ocean freight rate declines induce an equally dramatic fall in price gaps for traded commodities? They did *within* national markets. For example, the regional price convergence within the United States was dramatic: the wheat price gap between New York City and Iowa fell from 69 to 19 percent between 1870 and 1910, and from 52 to 10 percent between New York City and Wisconsin (Williamson 1974: 259). The price gaps *between* members of the Atlantic economy also tended to evaporate. Liverpool wheat prices exceeded Chicago prices by 58 percent in 1870, by 18 percent in 1895, and by 16 percent in 1912. Both the Liverpool–New York (figure 2.2) and New York–Chicago price gaps declined, which is consistent with the drop in freight rates. Moreover, these estimates *understate* the size of the price conver-

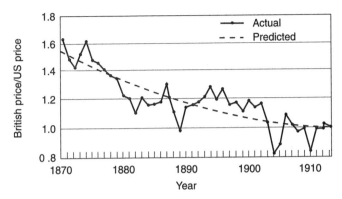

Figure 2.2 Anglo-American wheat price gap, 1870–1913
Source: O'Rourke and Williamson (1997a, figure 2.7).

gence because they ignore the collapse in price gaps between mid-western farm-gate and railhead, or between farm-gate and the docks in Buenos Aires and Odessa.

The experience in Anglo-American wheat markets was repeated for other foodstuffs. The second biggest tradeable foodstuff consisted of meat and animal fats such as beef, pork, mutton, and butter. The London–Cincinnati price differentials for bacon converged late, but after 1895 the convergence was even more dramatic than was true of wheat: price gaps were 92 percent in 1895 and 18 percent in 1913. The price convergence delay for meat, butter, and cheese has an easy explanation: it required the advances in refrigeration made toward the end of the century.

Anglo-American price data are also available for many other non-agricultural commodities (O'Rourke and Williamson 1994). The Boston–Manchester cotton textile price gap fell from 14 percent in 1870 to almost zero in 1913; the Philadelphia–London iron bar price gap fell from 75 to 21 percent, the pig iron gap fell from 85 to 19 percent, and the copper gap fell from 33 percent to zero; the Boston–London hides price gap fell from 28 to 9 percent, while the wool price gap fell from 59 to 28 percent. Commodity price convergence can also be documented for coal, tin, and coffee. International transport costs were also declining within Europe. For example, Anglo-Swedish price gaps for vegetable products fell from about 55 percent in 1876 to about 18 percent in 1910; animal products fell from about 40 percent to almost zero; and forestry products fell from about 145 to 70 percent (O'Rourke and Williamson 1995). Grain price convergence can be documented for a broader sample of European countries (O'Rourke 1997a), but I think this is sufficient to establish the point.

2.3 Did the subsequent trade boom cause living standard convergence?

The dramatic decline in transport costs across the late nineteenth century led to a trade boom and commodity price convergence across countries. Shortly after World War I, two Swedish economists looked back on the episode and argued that globalization in the form of commodity price convergence also had important income distribution implications for participating Atlantic economy members: Eli Heckscher, an economic historian, and Bertil Ohlin, a trade theorist, argued that commodity price convergence implied factor price convergence. Ohlin used an Old World versus New World example to illustrate the point:

> If, for example, Australia produced its own industrial products rather than importing them from Europe and America in exchange for agricultural products, then, on the one hand, the demand for labor would be greater and wages consequently higher, and, on the other, the demand for land, and therefore rent, lower than at present. At the same time, in Europe the scarcity of land would be greater and that of labor less than at present if the countries of Europe were constrained to produce for themselves all their agricultural products instead of importing some of them from abroad. Thus trade increases the price of land in Australia and lowers it in Europe, while tending to keep wages down in Australia and up in Europe. The tendency, in other words, is to approach an equalization of the prices of productive factors.
>
> (Ohlin 1924, in Flam and Flanders 1991: 91–92)

While Ohlin was talking about factor price convergence (e.g., "tendencies") not equalization, this statement marks the birth of the factor proportions approach and the factor price equalization theorem that continue to dominate trade theory to this day. They still inform public debate, as the ongoing controversy about the impact of globalization on real wages and inequality in the OECD testifies. The modern debate asks whether the trade boom between the industrialized OECD and the developing Third World is leading to increased wage inequality in labor-scarce countries, by forcing down the prices of goods intensive in unskilled labor, which can be more efficiently produced in the labor-abundant Third World. Symmetry suggests that the current trade boom also leads to rising wages and more equality in the Third World. Adrian Wood (1994) has made this Heckscher–Ohlin argument most forcefully, but most economists feel that the modern evidence fails to support this view of globalization's impact.

Perhaps history can help resolve the debate. Were Heckscher and Ohlin right about the late nineteenth-century trade boom? If the answer is based on *relative* factor prices, then they were unambiguously right. Table 1.2 (col. 2) shows wage–rental ratios rising steeply in Europe and falling steeply in the New World, and, furthermore, that they were falling more in those European economies that stayed open (like Britain) and less in those that stayed closed (like Spain). As a consequence, conditions improved for the poor unskilled worker relative to the rich landlord in much of Europe, while the opposite was true of the New World. Correlation is not causation, of course, but when the evidence is analyzed either econometrically or with computable general equilibrium models, Heckscher and Ohlin are shown to have been right (O'Rourke and Williamson 1994; O'Rourke, Taylor, and Williamson 1996; Williamson 1996; O'Rourke and Williamson 1997a: chapter 3). This is not to say that globalization through trade was the only force at work causing relative factor price convergence after 1870. For the Atlantic economy as a whole, globalization through trade probably did not account for more than a quarter of the wage–rental ratio convergence. The last chapter will return to the relative factor price and inequality issue.

The Heckscher–Ohlin model can also be used to help explain the convergence of absolute factor prices. Thus, it should help account for the convergence in real wages and living standards in the Atlantic economy from mid century to World War I. Global commodity market integration and trade booms should have led to factor price convergence, as countries everywhere expanded the production and export of commodities which used their abundant (and cheap) factor intensively. Thus, the demand for labor should have boomed in the low-wage countries and sagged in the high-wage countries, helping generate real wage convergence. When computable general equilibrium models are applied to the United States and Britain, it turns out that Heckscher and Ohlin are shown to be right. That is, one study found that globalization through trade accounted for as much as two-thirds of the Anglo-American real wage convergence between 1870 and 1895 (O'Rourke and Williamson 1994). It also found that these globalization forces were equally strong after 1895, but that they were overwhelmed by the more powerful divergent forces set in motion by industrial failure in Britain and industrial success in America. Technology mattered more after 1895 even in the Anglo-American case. But still, Heckscher and Ohlin were right in the Anglo-American case, and other studies using both CGEs (O'Rourke, Williamson, and Hatton 1994) and econometric methods (O'Rourke, Taylor, and Williamson 1996) have confirmed it.

But what about the rest of the Atlantic economy? It turns out that these effects were much weaker elsewhere, and the reason is that the textbook version of the Heckscher–Ohlin model simplifies too much to expect it to account for the wage and living standard convergence in the Atlantic economy more generally. Real wages and living standards were influenced by the combined effect of nominal wages in the numerator and living costs in the denominator. Given that fact, there are two reasons why globalization did not imply the same labor-market shock everywhere in the labor-abundant and land-scarce parts of the Atlantic economy. First, each country had a different economic structure, and so identical price shocks did not necessarily have the same effect on wages. Second, the price shocks associated with globalization through trade were not everywhere the same. These two considerations help explain why globalization through trade did not have the same impact on economy-wide real wages in Britain or Denmark, who stuck with free trade, compared with France, Germany, or Sweden, who reverted to protection.

Take the second reason first. The key point has to do with the behavior of price gaps between domestic and world markets, or between the import-competing industry at home and the export industry abroad (O'Rourke 1997a; O'Rourke and Williamson 1997a: chapter 5). Denmark was a free trader, but experienced far less price convergence in food products *vis-à-vis* the United States than did Britain. Trans-Atlantic integration may have lowered European grain prices, but intra-European integration raised grain prices in traditional grain-exporting countries such as Denmark. The result was that while average real cereal prices fell by 29 percent in Britain between 1870 and 1913, they fell by only 10 percent in Denmark over the same period. In contrast, under free trade French and German grain prices would have declined by 34 percent while Swedish prices would have declined by 27 percent. However, these three countries rejected free trade and turned instead to protection. If the grain invasion lowered grain prices by less in Denmark and in those parts of continental Europe that turned to protection, then it lowered workers' cost of living by less, and thus, *ceteris paribus*, raised real wages by less as well. Moreover, globalization also raised the prices of Scandinavian animal products, exported to the British market. Since refrigerated shipping only started eroding trans-Atlantic meat price gaps from the 1890s onwards, Scandinavian exports of bacon and dairy products were largely immune from New World competition for much of the late nineteenth century. In short, globalization through trade did not have identical effects on prices around the Atlantic economy.

Second, identical price shocks would have had very different effects on real wages, depending on a country's structure of production. Agriculture was relatively small in countries like Britain, an industrial leader. Britain also had a more capital-intensive agriculture, another attribute of industrial leadership. When CGE models for late nineteenth-century Britain, France, and Sweden are used to explore what would have happened if each country had experienced the same 29 percent decline in real grain prices that Britain did, very different results emerge: cheap grain *increased* British real wages, but, in the absence of tariffs, it would have reduced French real wages, while Swedish real wages would have stayed pretty much the same (O'Rourke 1997a). These differences can be easily interpreted in the context of the sector-specific factors model. Cheap grain lowered workers' cost of living economy wide, but it also reduced nominal wages since the demand for agricultural labor fell more than it rose elsewhere in the economy (agriculture usually being more labor intensive). Whether the cost-of-living effect or the nominal wage effect dominated economy wide depended on the size of agriculture. Only 23 percent of the British labor force worked in agriculture in 1871, while the figure for France was 51 percent. A negative shock to agricultural labor demand thus had a much bigger negative impact on French nominal wages economy wide than British, while the fall in the workers' cost of living was the same. Globalization through trade raised British real wages and helped erase the Anglo-American wage gap, but it did not do the same for the Franco-American wage gap.

These economic arguments help explain why globalization through trade fails to explain much of late nineteenth-century real wage convergence in the Atlantic economy, although it explains much of the Anglo-American convergence. Indeed, when the econometric analysis is done, globalization through trade can be shown to explain no more than a tenth of real wage and living standard convergence in the Atlantic economy up to 1914. Heckscher and Ohlin may have gotten the sign right, but they were not very relevant when it came to magnitudes. The history between 1870 and 1913 seems to be consistent with the consensus among modern economists that globalization through trade after 1970 simply has not mattered much in accounting for convergence between countries or for changes in income distribution within countries (Freeman 1995; Robbins 1996).

If globalization through trade did not matter much in the past, what about globalization through factor markets, and mass migrations in particular?

2.4 The impact of mass migrations: an overview

Given their enormous volume and ubiquity around the Atlantic economy, surely the pre-1914 mass migrations had a significant impact on labor markets at home, raising real wages, improving living standards, and eroding the poverty of those who stayed behind. And, just as surely, the mass migrations must also have had a significant impact on labor markets abroad: compared with a counterfactual world without them, the arrival of new immigrants must have reduced real wages, lowered living standards, and raised the poverty incidence for unskilled native-born and previous immigrant workers with whom the new arrivals competed. Thus, mass migration must have been a force tending to create economic convergence among the participating countries, living standards in the poor emigrating countries in Europe being pushed up closer to living standards in rich industrial countries in Europe and in immigrating countries overseas. Not all countries in the Atlantic economy participated, some had more induced catch-up than others, and some experienced other events which offset the migration forces, but the underlying tendencies must have been pervasive. The question is: how much? Did the mass migrations matter in an important way, and did observers at that time see it that way?

The remainder of this chapter will start by offering some evidence from two important emigrating countries which exhibited impressive catch-up – Ireland and Sweden. It will then explore the same issue for the biggest immigrant labor market of them all, the United States. What about all the rest? How big was the impact of the mass migrations on the Atlantic economy as a whole? It appears that the magnitudes were very large. The estimated contribution is so large, in fact, that its impact on convergence must have been partially offset by a variety of countervailing forces: independent disequilibrating forces of technical change (faster in some rich countries, like the United States and Canada); and dependent offsetting forces of capital-accumulation (international capital chasing after the migrants or native capital accumulation stimulated by the presence of immigrants), of natural resource exploitation (land settlement by migrants or by natives whom the migrants displaced in settled areas), of trade (migrant labor favoring the expansion of labor-intensive activities in rich countries), or of productivity gains (migrant-labor-induced scale economies). While these partial offsets must have been many and subtle, mass migration still made an unambiguous and profound contribution to economic convergence and to global labor-market integration prior to World War I.

2.5   Mass migration as a solution to problems at home

European emigration generated no shortage of political debate and moral judgment. Some Irish post-famine commentators, for example, viewed the emigrant flood as the result of Ireland's failure to industrialize and thus its inability to create enough good jobs (ÓGráda 1994: chapter 13). Others saw the flood in even more negative terms, as one more *cause* of industrial failure. One worry was that these emigrations drained the home country of the best and brightest, jeopardizing the future. Such emigrant self-selection might help explain Ireland's inability to attract foreign capital, despite its low wages (Mokyr 1991; O'Rourke 1992). Another argument was that Ireland failed to industrialize because its home market was too small; once too small, scale economies were hard to achieve, Irish manufacturing lost its competitive edge, and industrial job creation faltered; emigrants fled the stagnant Irish labor market; and the market got even smaller. Such commentary would imply that a dismal path-dependent historical process was at work which ensured Irish industrial failure (ÓGráda 1994: 342–347), an argument that sounds like those offered by the new economic geography to explain modern divergence (Krugman and Venables 1995). Of course, this argument ignores the fact that there was an enormous British market close by which Ireland could and did exploit by trade.

There is some evidence from pre-famine Ireland that emigration may have implied a human capital loss to the economy, providing other nations with "instant adults" reared at Ireland's expense (Neal and Uselding 1972; Mokyr and ÓGráda 1982; Williamson 1997b), and some evidence that the better educated and more highly skilled were those who left (Nicholas and Shergold 1987). However, while post-famine Ireland certainly experienced industrial failure, it *did*, as we have seen, undergo an impressive real wage catch-up on both Britain and America. Economics as old as that of Adam Smith can explain why: emigration made labor more scarce in Ireland, thus raising real wages, and living standards at home, both in absolute terms and relative to immigrant nations. This kind of Smithian economics exploits diminishing returns: given land, capital, and technology, more labor means lower productivity, real wages, and living standards; less labor means higher productivity, real wages and living standards. While the movers may have been able to escape to higher wages abroad, the now-scarcer stayers found conditions improving at home – not as much as the improvement captured by the emigrants of course, but improvements nonetheless.

Swedish commentators also viewed emigration as a sign of failure: surely, they seemed to have said, it is a poor economy that cannot generate enough good jobs to keep young men at home. The Swedes left in especially large numbers in the 1880s, and the debate became most intense right about that time. And they debated in spite of the fact that Sweden and the rest of the Scandinavian economies were in the midst of the most impressive European catch-up by far, a catch-up which, in contrast with Ireland, seemed to be carried by vigorous industrialization (O'Rourke and Williamson 1995, 1996, 1997b). In 1882, Knut Wicksell, a young theorist and neo-Malthusian, wrote a popular essay which argued the Smithian case: emigration would eventually solve the pauper problem which blighted labor-abundant and land-scarce Swedish agriculture and thus was a good thing to be tolerated, perhaps even stimulated.

What *was* the impact of mass emigration on the home country? The literature is loud on assertion but quiet on evidence, even though more than a century has passed since Wicksell's essay appeared. I will deal with Wicksell's Sweden in a moment, but first I turn to Ireland, where, after all, the European mass migrations started.

2.6 The impact of mass emigration on irish labor markets

Estimates of Irish national income for the late nineteenth century are sketchy, but Cormac ÓGráda (1994: 242, 379) uses what we have to guess that Irish national income grew at about 0.7 percent

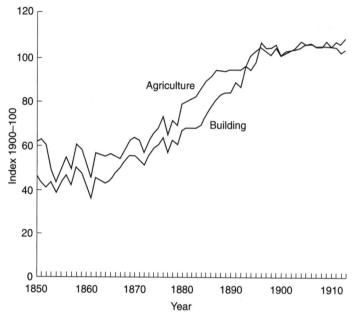

Figure 2.3 Irish real wage rate, 1850–1913
Source: Boyer, Halton, and O'Rourke (1994, figure 9.1).

per annum between 1845 and 1913. Per capita income grew more than twice as fast, 1.6 percent per annum. That is not a typographical error: per capita income grew a lot faster than did total income since the Irish population fell over the period. Per capita income growth is somewhat slower if we skip over the famine, say about 1.3 percent per annum. Irish income per capita rose from about two-fifths to about three-fifths of Britain from the mid century to World War I. Furthermore, the share of the population in poverty declined and the families living in what was classed as lowest-quality housing dropped from 63 percent in 1861 to 29 percent 50 years later (Hatton and Williamson 1993).

Although GNP per capita and other indicators of well-being suggest significant improvement, it can, as the first chapter reported, also be documented by real wages, information more directly relevant in describing the labor-market conditions which were driving emigrants abroad and in describing the market which had to adjust most to their departure. Figure 2.3

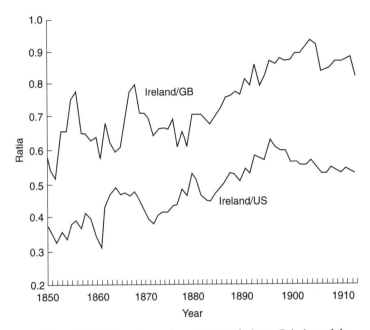

Figure 2.4 Irish urban real wage rates relative to Britain and the
United States, 1850–1913
Source: Boyer, Halton, and O'Rourke, (1994, figure 9.2).

plots the real wage for Irish building and agricultural laborers.
Two features stand out. First, the two indices move closely
together over the whole period, suggesting that the Irish
unskilled labor market was fairly well integrated. Second, both
series exhibit substantial real wage growth (as do the alternative
Irish real wage estimates in tables 1.2 and 2.2). Between 1855 and
1913 real wages more than doubled, an observation consistent
with the available evidence on the growth of national income per
capita. Third, most of the growth is concentrated in the period
between 1860 and 1895.

The trends in Irish real wages can be compared with those in
the major receiving countries, Britain and the United States, using
the same purchasing power parity adjusted wage rates discussed
in the previous chapter. Figure 2.4 plots the ratios for building
laborers: Irish wages rose from about 60 percent of British wages
in the early 1850s to about 85 percent after the turn of the century,

while over the same period they rose from about 35 percent to about 55 percent of American wages. Given that Ireland did not industrialize rapidly during the period, and given that the Irish population declined, it is tempting to conclude that the labor force contraction was the main source of the convergence. This appeal to Smithian reasoning – an easing of pressure on the land – is certainly consistent with the relative rise in Irish wages and a decline in the rural labor surplus.

Most of the decline in the Irish population and labor force between the Great Famine and World War I took place in rural areas and on the farm. Between 1851 and 1913 the rural population fell by over 2.6 million, a decline of almost one half. Meanwhile, the population living in towns and cities rose by about a half million, so that the share living in urban areas more than doubled, jumping from 12 to 29 percent. In fact, only two of the 32 Irish counties experienced a population increase over the six decades, the urban counties of Dublin and Antrim.

In short, economic conditions facing Irish laborers improved dramatically in the half century following the famine not only in absolute terms but relative to Britain and the United States. These facts are certainly supportive of the hypothesis that the real wage in post-famine Ireland was being driven by the size of the labor force, and thus that the wage was intimately tied to emigration. While supportive, the hypothesis needs reinforcement. After all, the economics is very simple and population is unlikely to be a perfect proxy for the labor force. We need to estimate the impact of emigration on the labor force and we need a more explicit model to measure its effects.

Enormous labor force shocks such as the Irish exodus can best be assessed by a general equilibrium framework which allows for the full set of influences felt throughout the domestic economy. What follows relies on a computable general equilibrium (CGE) model of the 1907–1908 Irish economy, designed to assess the effects of post-famine emigration on Irish real wages and living standards (Boyer, Hatton, and O'Rourke 1994). In a moment, I will report the results when a similar model is applied to Sweden.

How much of the post-famine rise in real wages was due to emigration? To get the answer, George Boyer, Timothy Hatton, and Kevin O'Rourke (1994) estimated how much bigger the 1907–1908 Irish labor force would have been in a world of no emigration from 1851 onwards. They then used the 1907–1908 model to calculate what wages would have been in this counterfactual no-emigration world. This gave them an estimate of the independent impact of the post-famine Irish emigration on labor markets at home. Furthermore, their Irish model allowed trade to have an offsetting impact on real wages, just as Heckscher and Ohlin insisted: changes in labor scarcity induced by emigrations abroad can change output mix (Ireland can produce less labor-intensive products) and trade patterns (Ireland can shift into less labor-intensive exports). These endogenous changes in economic activity and trade will tend to diminish, but not eliminate, the impact of rising labor scarcity on real wages and living standards.

What about world capital markets? Cannot capital flows serve as a substitute for Irish emigration by moving in the opposite direction? If emigration had been only a trickle from a labor surplus area like Ireland, would not capital have flooded in to exploit the cheap labor? Since Irish emigration was actually a flood, should not capital have retreated from the now more expensive labor-market area? Cormac ÓGráda (1994: chapters 12–14) makes a persuasive case that capital was mobile over Irish borders prior to World War I. But exactly how mobile? We do not know, so all I can do is offer two extreme cases, expecting the truth to lie somewhere in between: one where the rental rate on capital is taken as exogenous implying that small Ireland could have borrowed (or loaned) as much additional capital as it wished from (to) world capital markets (e.g., London) without influencing the world interest rate, and one where Ireland had to go it alone and thus could not have borrowed (or loaned) any additional capital from (to) foreign markets.

In the internationally immobile capital case, Boyer, Hatton, and O'Rourke (1994) estimate that the real wage in agriculture was 19–40 percent higher as a result of emigration, while the non-farm wage was 24–52 percent higher. Per capita GNP rose by 15–33 percent due to emigration. Thus, wages rose by more than per capita income due to emigration. This result certainly confirms who gained and who lost from emigration. Workers who stayed behind gained, since increasing labor scarcity raised wages. Landlords lost, since increasing labor scarcity cut into their rents: rents were reduced by 33–54 percent due to emigration. Capitalists lost, since increasing labor scarcity cut into their profits: rates of return on capital were reduced by 28–45 percent.

Suppose, instead, that capital was completely mobile over Irish borders. What then? While still big, all of the effects of emigration just discussed would have been somewhat smaller. In the absence of emigration, more labor and lower wages would have attracted more foreign capital (or kept more Irish capital at home); more foreign capital would have meant better equipped Irish workers than in the capital immobile case; and thus the glut of workers in the counterfactual world without emigration would have been at least partially offset by more capital.[1] Under the capital mobile case, both farm and non-farm wages increase by 6–12 percent as a result of emigration, not the 19–52 percent seen in the capital immobile case. The average of all of these emigration-induced wage increases is about 21 percent.

These figures imply that post-famine Irish emigration may have accounted for as much as a half of the real wage growth and a third of the income per capita growth observed. It also explains a large share of Irish catch-up on the leaders abroad: emigration accounts for a third of Irish convergence on Britain and the United States even if capital is assumed mobile.

Irish emigration by itself made a powerful contribution to Irish real wage and living standards convergence on Britain and the United States. What happens when US immigration (some of which was Irish) is added to the story? Later in this chapter, we will find that, in the absence of immigration after 1870, the 1910 US population might have been around 17 percent smaller than it actually was, and the 1910 labor force around 24 percent smaller. According to CGE counterfactual analysis, unskilled urban real

---

[1] Even perfect capital mobility is only a partial offset. After all, more capital and labor in the no-emigration world would have to work with the same amount of land. This would be especially important in poor agrarian economies like Ireland, Sweden, and other emigrating countries, where (fixed) land endowments were important inputs to economy-wide output performance.

wages would have been about 9 percent higher, in which case all of the post-famine Irish convergence on the United States was due to mass migration.[2]

2.7 The impact of mass emigration on Swedish labor markets

The first chapter documented that Ireland, Scandinavia, and even Italy underwent catch-up from the Great Famine to World War I. The performance of the Scandinavian countries was particularly impressive: per capita income, real wages, and average labor productivity grew faster in Denmark, Norway, Sweden, and even Finland than in the rest of north-western Europe (table 1.2). Thus, the gap between the Scandinavian late-comers and Britain narrowed considerably. To offer just two examples: between 1870 and 1910, Swedish labor productivity rose from 39 to 53 percent of British; over the same forty years, Danish unskilled urban real wages rose from 52 to 96 percent of British. Indeed, real wages in Scandinavia even rose relative to fast-growing America: in Norway urban unskilled real wages rose from 25 to 43 percent of the United States, while those in Sweden rose from 30 to 59 percent of the United States.

This rapid Scandinavian catch-up is now well documented by evidence which was unavailable to observers at that time, but it was apparent to Swedish economists writing in the middle or at the end of the period – like Knut Wicksell, Eli Heckscher, and Bertil Ohlin. The amazing aspect of the literature on the Scandinavian catch-up is that until recently no one tried to assess its sources. There has been no shortage of assertion, of course, ranging from schooling advantages, favorable price shocks, the right natural resource endowment, trade creation, mass emigration, and elastic foreign capital inflows. Kevin O'Rourke and I recently put

---

[2] The same was not true for Anglo-Ireland since Britain recorded high emigration rates, too: in the absence of emigration, British wages would have been about 5 percent lower. Thus, allowing for the impact of migrations on the two leaders strengthens migration's contribution to Irish real wage convergence on the United States but weakens it on British.

some empirical content into those assertions (O'Rourke and Williamson 1995, 1996, 1997b).

What contribution did Scandinavian emigration make? As I pointed out above, Knut Wicksell asserted a century ago that emigration would solve the pauper problem which blighted Swedish agriculture. His pro-emigration agitation was followed by other voices in the 1890s, including Adrian Molin and Gustav Sundbarg. Tests of Wicksell's assertion were very slow in coming despite the intensity of the debate on the economic impact of the late nineteenth-century mass migrations.

There are two questions one can pose of the late nineteenth-century mass migrations. How much of Swedish (Norwegian or Danish) real wage and labor productivity growth can be assigned to emigration, the out-migrations having created more labor scarcity at home? How much of the Swedish (Norwegian or Danish) catch-up can be assigned more generally to mass migration, both the emigrations from poor Sweden and the immigrations (of Swedes and non-Swedes) into the rich New World, like the United States (where most of the Swedes and the rest of the Scandinavian emigrants went)? What about Swedish catch-up on Britain who herself was an emigrant country? My interest is in the last two catching-up questions, but as we saw in the Irish analysis each of these questions employ the same methodology to get the answers: estimate the labor force in a counterfactual no-migration environment for both the rich and poor country; with the counterfactual labor force estimate in hand, assess the impact of the altered labor force on living standards and productivity by the application of some model of the rich and poor economies; finally, compute the share of the measured living standards and productivity catch-up explained by the mass migrations.

So, I start with the first question: Did emigration have a big impact on the labor force at home? Scandinavian emigration rates reached their peak in the 1880s, and at that time they were among the highest in Europe, exceeded only by Ireland and the rest of the United Kingdom. The rate for the decade was 95.2 per thousand of the population in Norway, 70.1 per thousand in Sweden, and 39.4 per thousand in Denmark (Hatton and Williamson 1997: table 2.1): Sweden lay in the middle of the

Scandinavian range. Emigration went through booms and busts, but by 1910 the Danish population was 11 percent below what it would have been in the absence of the emigrations over the four decades following 1870, the Swedish population was 15 percent lower and the Norwegian population 19 percent lower (table 2.1). Since emigration favored young adults with high labor participation rates, the impact on the home labor force was even bigger than on the home population. Thus, the Swedish labor force was about 20 percent smaller in 1910 than it would have been in the absence of emigration. The influence of emigration on Sweden and the rest of Scandinavia was far from trivial.

Kevin O'Rourke and I report the cumulative impact of Swedish emigration 1870–1910 on Swedish real wages in 1910 (O'Rourke and Williamson 1995, 1997b). In contrast with the Irish analysis above, the immobile capital case is not explored here: capital inflows into Sweden over these four decades were very large in spite of Swedish emigration; it is hard to imagine that they would have been even larger in the absence of emigration, so I ignore the possibility. In terms of labor-market impact, emigration between 1870 and 1910 served to raise urban wages in Sweden by about 12 percent above what they would have been in its absence. Urban unskilled wages in Sweden actually increased by 191 percent over the four decades, so the 12 percent looks pretty small by comparison. Granted, Wicksell was talking about agricultural poverty, but the impact of emigration on farm wages was also "only" 12 percent, hardly enough to confirm Wicksell's optimism that emigration would solve the pauper problem in Swedish agriculture. Other events mattered far more, it seems.

What about as a share of the catch-up with Britain or the United States? The impact of mass migration on the rapidly contracting wage gap between Britain and Sweden was small, certainly no more than a tenth of the catch-up. The reason for the small contribution is clear: Britain recorded an emigration rate not too far below that of Sweden (and the rest of Scandinavia). Once again, Wicksell seems to have been wrong: emigration did not make a significant contribution to Anglo-Swedish catch-up. But what about Swedish catch-up with the United States, the country which absorbed 98 percent of the Swedish overseas emigrants?[3] As we shall see below, the immigration rate in the late nineteenth-century United States was enormous, and its cumulative impact from 1870 onwards was to make the 1910 labor force 24 percent bigger than it would have been in its absence, making real wages 9 percent lower than they would have been without the immigration. The mass migration had a big impact on the rapidly contracting wage gap between the United States and Sweden, explaining about four-tenths of the Swedish catch-up on the United States.

2.8 Absorbing the immigrants: the impact on American labor markets

The impact of the immigrants on American labor markets obsessed contemporary observers, and it was discussed at length in the famous Immigration Commission Report of 1911. Here I confront three questions that are just as relevant today as they were almost a century ago: Where did the immigrants find employment? Did the immigrants crowd out natives? Did the increased foreign-born presence significantly reduce native workers' wages?

On the issue of employment location, we can discriminate between two views. The first view is optimistic: it argues that the immigrants entered rapidly growing, high-wage employment thereby easing short-run labor supply bottlenecks in leading industries. The second view is pessimistic: it argues that immigrants crowded into slow-growing, low-wage employment in industries undergoing relative decline, thereby crowding out unskilled natives. These competing views can be examined by comparing the share of immigrants in a given occupation with employment growth in that occupation. If that share was high and rising in rapidly expanding industries and occupations, and controlling for other factors, then immigrants could be regarded

---

[3] The United States absorbed 90 percent of the Danish emigrants and 97 percent of the Norwegian emigrants.

as the "shock troops" of structural change.[4] Timothy Hatton and I examined evidence from the 1890s and confirmed that immigrants found employment more frequently in unskilled jobs, compared with natives (Hatton and Williamson 1997: chapter 8). New immigrant arrivals tended to be unskilled. More to the point, immigrants tended to locate more frequently than natives in slow-growth sectors, not fast-growth sectors. Furthermore, the foreign-born share tended to fall most in the fastest-growing occupations and least in the slowest-growing occupations. In short, there is no evidence to support the view that the foreign-born dominated fast-growing parts of the US economy prior to World War I. Nor is there any evidence to support the view that immigrants flowed disproportionately into high-growth sectors and occupations. In fact, the evidence suggests the contrary: immigrants flowed disproportionately into the slowest-growing occupations.

There is a ready explanation for these facts: given that occupational growth reflects shifting comparative advantage, and given that the United States was exploiting its comparative advantage in resource- and capital-intensive industries, it follows that fast-growing sectors should have generated buoyant demand growth for skilled labor (a complement with capital) and sluggish demand growth for unskilled labor (a substitute for capital). Thus, unskilled immigrants *should* have flooded into unskilled-labor-intensive industries and occupations where growth was slower. Indeed, these findings are consistent with those from the 1980s and 1990s (Baumol *et al.* 1989; Borjas 1994), when the flood of new less-skilled immigrants into services and import-competing manufacturing has raised the same concern that New York's immigrant ghettos and sweatshops did in the 1890s. The evidence from the 1890s also seems to confirm a mis-match between labor demand, which was shifting away from unskilled occupations (e.g., becoming more skilled), and booming immigrant labor supplies that were declining in quality (e.g., becoming less skilled). It

---

[4] The term comes from Sidney Pollard (1978) who characterized the Irish in early industrializing Britain the same way. Williamson (1986) disagreed. The exchange between Pollard and Williamson over the impact of the Irish immigrants on British workers from the 1820s to the 1850s exactly parallels this later debate in America.

had, of course, inequality implications then (Williamson and Lindert 1980; Williamson 1982, 1997a) just as it does now (Borjas, Freeman, and Katz 1992). It crowded out native unskilled workers (including southern blacks) and thus widened the gap between the working poor and the rest. In this sense, the 1911 Congress, reading the Immigration Commission Report, and today's Congress, reading gloomy news in *The Economist* on rising inequality, share the same concern. I will return to these issues in the next chapter.

What I have said about occupations need not, of course, apply to regions. Surely immigrants moved into the most rapidly expanding states, thus easing excess demand in local labor markets. Once again Hatton and I supplied an answer (Hatton and Williamson 1997: chapter 8). Looking at the proportion of foreign-born for the intercensal periods 1880–1890, 1890–1900, and 1900–1910, we were able to show that north-eastern states whose populations grew rapidly experienced a significant rise in foreign-born density. This reflects the well-known fact that immigrants moved to the cities in the most rapidly growing states on the eastern seaboard. In contrast, however, the more rapid was the growth of a state's population in the west north central or mountain region, the more the foreign-born share *fell*. Thus, while immigrants moved disproportionately into the most rapidly growing centers on the east coast, they did not do so elsewhere in the US. These facts raise a relevant question about "push" and "pull." Did immigrants crowd out natives in fast-growing east coast labor markets thus pushing them west? Or, did the westward movement of natives pull foreign immigrants into east coast labor markets? When the spatial analysis takes proper account of labor demand, it seems clear that immigrants were indeed crowding out unskilled natives on the urban east coast (Hatton and Williamson 1997: table 8.5; Collins 1997). Immigrant and native unskilled workers were substitutes, not complements.

The key immigrant absorption question, however, has always been whether today's unskilled immigrants lowered the wage rates and living standards of natives and yesterday's immigrants with whom they competed. In one recent study, Claudia Goldin (1994) estimated the correlation between immigration and wage changes across cities between 1890 and 1915. She found that a one percentage point increase in the foreign-born population share reduced unskilled wage rates by about 1–1.5 percent. True, her objective was to identify local relative wage impacts rather than to infer the economy-wide effect of immigration. But local labor-market studies almost certainly understate (or miss entirely) the economy-wide impact of immigration on wages. After all, immigration will only lower wages in a local labor market insofar as it increases the total supply of labor. If there is instead completely offsetting native emigration then a rise in the immigrant share is consistent with no change in the size of the local labor force, and no wage effect of immigration compared with other local labor markets in which natives relocate. But wages should fall in all locations (perhaps equally, perhaps not). These effects are not measured by local labor-market studies if local labor markets are well connected.

Another way to examine the impact of immigration on the real wage is to estimate the wage adjustment mechanism from time-series data. By altering labor supply and unemployment in the short run, immigration should drive down the wage along some long-run Phillips curve. Hatton and I estimated such a model on annual observations for 1890–1913 (Hatton and Williamson 1997: table 8.6). The long-run solution to the estimated model suggests that, holding output constant, an increase in the labor force by 1 percent lowered the real wage in the long run by 0.4 or 0.5 percent. Based on the stock of foreign-born and their children enumerated in the 1910 census, immigration after 1870 accounted for about 27 percent of the 1910 labor force.[5] These magnitudes suggest that the 1910 real wage would have been 11 to 14 percent higher in the absence of immigration after 1870.

These time-series results are consistent with those based on CGE models. For example, the first effort to apply computable general equilibrium techniques to the late nineteenth-century United States estimated that immigration after 1870 lowered real wages in 1910 by 11 percent (Williamson 1974: 387), almost iden-

---

[5] The slightly smaller labor-market effects cited in table 2.1 for the United States exclude the children of the foreign born (24 percent in 1910), while they are included here (27 percent in 1910).

tical to the time-series estimate.[6] More recently, another CGE experiment, which allowed capital to chase after labor, got pretty much the same result: immigration reduced real wages in 1910 by about 9 percent (O'Rourke, Williamson, and Hatton 1994: 209), a figure confirmed in table 2.1 below.

2.9 The impact of mass migration on the Atlantic economy

The first lecture showed that real wages and living standards converged among the currently industrialized OECD countries between 1870 and World War I. The convergence was driven primarily by the erosion of the average wage gap between the New World and the Old, but many poor European countries caught up, at least in part, with the industrial leaders. How much of this convergence was due to mass migration? How much was due to other forces like trade-induced factor-price convergence, resource accumulation, and productivity advance? So far, I have appealed to the experience of one immigrant country – the United States – and two emigrant countries – Ireland and Sweden, to illustrate the potential strength of mass migrations on the evolution of an integrated Atlantic labor market between the 1860s and World War I. What about the rest of the Atlantic economy?[7]

Table 2.1 reports late nineteenth-century net migration rates for five New World and twelve Old World countries. In addition, the table assesses the cumulative labor force impact of these post-1870 migrations on each country in 1910. The impact varied greatly: Argentina's labor force was augmented most by immigration (86 percent), Brazil's the least (4 percent), with the United States lying in between (24 percent), the latter below the New World average of 40 percent; Ireland's labor force was diminished most by emigration (45 percent), France and The Netherlands the

---

[6] This result was also confirmed using a CGE for the 1890–1913 period (Williamson and Lindert 1980).

[7] This section draws heavily on Taylor and Williamson (1997). It should be noted that they use the Maddison 1991 GDP estimates, not his 1995 revisions, so tables 2.2 and 2.3 may differ a bit from the revised GDP estimates reported elsewhere in these lectures. It does not, however, effect the conclusion.

Table 2.1. *Summary data: net immigration rates and cumulative impact, 1870–1910*

	Persons Adjusted net migration rate 1870–1910 (per 1000)	*Persons* Adjusted cumulative poulation impact 1910 (per cent)	*Labor Force* Adjusted net migration rate 1870–1910 (per 1000)	*Labor Force* Adjusted cumulative labor force impact 1910 (per cent)
Argentina	11.74	60	15.50	86
Australia	6.61	30	8.73	42
Belgium	1.67	7	2.20	9
Brazil	0.74	3	0.98	4
Canada	6.92	32	9.14	44
Denmark	− 2.78	− 11	− 3.67	− 14
France	− 0.10	0	− 0.13	− 1
Germany	− 0.73	− 3	− 0.96	− 4
Great Britain	− 2.25	− 9	− 2.97	− 11
Ireland	− 11.24	− 36	− 14.84	− 45
Italy	− 9.25	− 31	− 12.21	− 39
Netherlands	− 0.59	− 2	− 0.78	− 3
Norway	− 5.25	− 19	− 6.93	− 24
Portugal	− 1.06	− 4	− 1.40	− 5
Spain	− 1.16	− 5	− 1.53	− 6
Sweden	− 4.20	− 15	− 5.55	− 20
United States	− 4.03	17	5.31	24
New World	6.01	29	7.93	40
Old World	− 3.08	− 11	− 4.06	− 13

Notes: Rates per thousand per annum. Minus denotes emigration.
Source: Taylor and Williamson 1997, table 1.

least (1 and 3 percent), with Britain lying in between (11 percent), the latter just a little below the Old World average of 13 percent. These, then, are the Atlantic economy mass migrations whose labor-market impact I wish to assess.

Table 2.2 shows exactly what it is I wish to explain. There I offer two measures of convergence across the late nineteenth century.

Table 2.2. *Summary data: convergence, 1870–1910*

	Real wages		GDP per capita		GDP per worker	
	1870	1910	1870	1910	1870	1910
Levels						
Argentina	61	95	915	2,226	1,946	5,317
Australia	127	135	3,123	4,586	7,811	10,573
Belgium	60	87	2,104	3,171	4,836	7,059
Brazil	39	85	425	549	1,101	1,422
Canada	99	205	1,365	3,263	3,781	7,876
Denmark	36	99	1,624	3,005	2,943	5,900
France	50	71	1,638	2,503	3,336	5,031
Germany	58	87	772	1,424	2,996	5,510
Great Britain	67	95	3,055	4,026	7,132	9,448
Ireland	49	91	—	—	—	—
Italy	26	50	1,244	1,933	2,309	3,290
Netherlands	57	77	2,064	2,964	5,322	7,795
Norway	32	79	1,190	1,875	2,800	4,719
Portugal	18	24	612	901	1,346	2,024
Spain	30	36	1,308	1,962	3,194	4,919
Sweden	28	100	1,316	2,358	2,814	5,019
United States	115	170	2,254	4,559	5,925	10,681
Dispersion (1870 = 100)						
All	100	72	100	82	100	71
New World	100	75	100	71	100	65
Old World	100	81	100	70	100	61
New World/Old World						
Gap (Parity = 100):						
	208	185	105	128	116	129

Notes: Dispersion measure is variance divided by the square of the mean (or CV squared), using an index with 1870 = 100.
Source: Taylor and Williamson 1997, table 3.

One measures the decline in the dispersion across the Atlantic economy, and one measures the decline in the gap between the New World and Old. Each of these is calculated for real wages, GDP per capita, and GDP per worker.

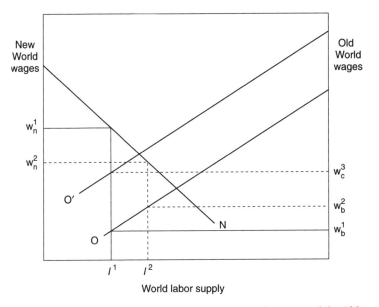

Figure 2.5 Allocating labor supplies between the New and the Old World

Like the CGE analyses reported earlier in this lecture, what follows also exploits the counterfactual. However, the model, though much simpler, was estimated econometrically. As before, the purpose is to assess migration's role in accounting for convergence, here measured by the decline in dispersion between 1870 and 1910. The relevant data are summarized in the middle panel of table 2.2: real wage dispersion declined by 28 percent over the period, GDP per capita dispersion by 18 percent, and GDP per worker dispersion by 29 percent. What contribution did international migration make to that measured convergence? To answer the question, I ask another: what would have been the measured convergence 1870–1910 had there been no migration?

The standard way of dealing with this question on the blackboard is illustrated by figure 2.5 where the answer is simplified by looking only at the wage gap between New World and Old World labor markets. New World wages and labor's marginal product are on the left-hand side and Old World wages and labor's marginal product are on the right-hand side. The world labor supply is measured along the horizontal axis. An equilibrium distribution of labor, of course, occurs at the intersection of the two derived labor demand schedules (O and N). Instead, I start at l^1 where labor is scarce in the New World, and thus where the wage gap between the two regions is very large, $w_n^1 - w_o^1$. If mass migrations redistribute labor toward the New World, say to l^2, the wage gap collapses to $w_n^2 - w_o^2$, and all the observed convergence would be attributable to migration. However, the same kind of convergence could have been achieved by a relative demand shift: a shift in O to O', an event driven perhaps by relative price shocks favoring labor in the Old World or by faster accumulation and technological change there. The no-migration counterfactual invokes the *ceteris paribus* assumption: the population and labor force are adjusted according to the average net migration (and labor participation) rate observed during the period, and assume that technology, capital stocks, prices, and all else remain constant. Such assumptions impart an upward bias on the measured impact of mass migration, but let us see whether the magnitudes for the Atlantic economy as a whole are large enough to warrant a debate over bias.

Migration affects long-run equilibrium output and wages to the extent that it influences aggregate labor supply. Alan Taylor and I estimated labor demand elasticities econometrically, and used these results to assess the wage impact of changing labor supply by country. Table 2.3 presents the results. The upper panel shows counterfactual real wages, GDP per capita, and GDP per worker all in 1910, had there been zero net migration after 1870 in all countries. The second panel indicates the proportionate impact of migration on real wages, and GDP per capita and per worker. The third panel reports counterfactual convergence or divergence.

The results certainly accord with intuition: in the absence of the mass migrations, wages and labor productivity would have been a lot higher in the New World and a lot lower in the Old; and, in the absence of the mass migrations, income per capita would typically (but not always) have been marginally higher in the New World and typically (but not always) marginally lower in the Old World. Not surprisingly, the biggest counterfactual impact is

Table 2.3. *Counterfactual convergence 1870–1910 with zero net migration*

	Real wages		GDP per capita		GDP per worker	
	1870	1910	1870	1910	1870	1910
Levels						
Argentina	61	121	915	2,424	1,946	6,730
Australia	127	158	3,123	4,920	7,811	12,346
Belgium	60	91	2,104	3,272	4,836	7,442
Brazil	39	87	425	552	1,101	1,444
Canada	99	243	1,365	3,533	3,781	9,318
Denmark	36	92	1,624	2,898	2,943	5,491
France	50	70	1,638	2,499	3,336	5,017
Germany	58	85	772	1,406	2,996	5,390
Great Britain	67	90	3,055	3,918	7,132	8,934
Ireland	49	69	-	-	-	-
Italy	26	39	1,244	1,692	2,309	3,048
Netherlands	57	75	2,064	2,931	5,322	7,649
Norway	32	72	1,190	1,818	2,800	4,276
Portugal	18	23	612	901	1,346	2,024
Spain	30	34	1,308	1,962	3,194	4,919
Sweden	28	93	1,316	2,300	2,814	4,639
United States	115	185	2,254	4,714	5,925	11,628
Change (counterfactual versus actual), %						
Argentina		27		9		27
Australia		17		7		17
Belgium		5		3		5
Brazil		2		1		2
Canada		18		8		18
Denmark		−7		−4		−7
France		0		0		0
Germany		−2		−1		−2
Great Britain		−5		−3		−5
Ireland		−24		−13		−24
Italy		−22		−12		−22
Netherlands		−2		−1		−2
Norway		−9		−3		−9
Portugal		−3		−2		−3
Spain		−3		−2		−3

Table 2.3 (*cont.*)

	Real wages		GDP per capita		GDP per worker	
	1870	1910	1870	1910	1870	1910
Sweden		−8		−2		−8
United States		9		3		9
Dispersion (1870 = 100)						
All						
New World	100	107	100	91	100	91
Old World	100	81	100	70	100	62
	100	87	100	73	100	69
New World/Old World:						
Gap (Parity = 100)	208	228	105	139	116	155

Notes: Dispersion measure and actual data as in table 2.2. On the counterfactual, see text.

Source: Taylor and Williamson 1997, table 4.

reported for those countries which experienced the biggest migrations: by 1910, Irish wages would have been lower by 24 percent, Italian by 22 percent, and Swedish by 8 percent; and Argentine wages would have been higher by 27 percent, Australian by 17 percent, Canadian by 18 percent, and American by 9 percent.

The partial equilibrium assessment in table 2.3 is higher than it would be in general equilibrium: after all, it ignores trade responses and changes in output mix, both of which would have muted the impact of the counterfactual no-migration impact; and it also ignores global capital-market responses, although this latter shortcoming will be repaired in a moment. Whether an overstatement or not, table 2.3 certainly lends strong support to the hypothesis that mass migration made an important contribution to late nineteenth-century convergence. Starting with the third panel first, we observe that in the absence of the mass migrations real wage dispersion would have *increased* by 7 percent, rather than decreased by 28 percent as it did in fact (compare tables 2.2 and 2.3). GDP per worker dispersion would have decreased by only 9 percent, rather than by 29 percent as it did in fact. GDP per capita dispersion would also have decreased by only 9 percent, rather than by 18 percent as it did in fact. Wage gaps between New World and Old in fact declined from 108 to 85 percent, but in the absence of the mass migrations they would have *risen* to 128 percent in 1910.

Pairwise comparisons are also easily constructed using table 2.3. Wage gaps between many Old World countries and the United States fell dramatically as a result of mass migration: without Irish emigration (some of whom went to America) and US immigration (some of whom were Irish), the American–Irish wage gap would have risen by 34 percentage points (from 134 to 168 percent), while in fact it fell by 48 (from 134 to 86 percent); without Italian emigration (a large share of whom went to America) and US immigration (many of whom were Italian), the American–Italian wage gap would have risen by 32 percentage points, while in fact it fell by 102; without British emigration and Australian immigration, the Australian–British wage gap would have fallen by 14 percentage points, while in fact it fell by 48; and without Italian emigration and Argentine immigration, the Argentine–Italian wage gap would have risen by 75 percentage points, while in fact it fell by 45. Furthermore, the mass migrations to the New World had an impact on economic convergence within the Old World: without the Norwegian emigration flood and the German emigration trickle, the German–Norwegian wage gap would have fallen by 116 percentage points, while in fact it fell by 122; and without the fact that Irish emigration exceeded British emigration by far, the British–Irish wage gap would have fallen only by 7 percentage points, while in fact it fell by 33. Although the impact of mass migration *within* the Old World appears to have been much smaller than that *between* the Old and New World, remember the caveat that migrations within Europe were underenumerated.

The counterfactual results in table 2.3 suggest that more than all (125 percent) of the real wage convergence 1870–1910 (log measure of dispersion) was attributable to migration, and almost three-quarters (70 percent) of the GDP per worker convergence. In contrast, perhaps one half (50 percent) of the GDP per capita convergence might have been due to migration.

The contribution of mass migration to convergence in the full sample and in the New and Old World differ, the latter being smaller and in two out of three New World cases even negative. Those negative numbers can be explained by the fact that the Atlantic labor market was segmented. Immigrant flows were not everywhere efficiently distributed, since barriers to entry limited destination choices for many southern Europeans. Thus migrants did not always obey some simple market-wage calculus; kept out of the best high-wage destinations, or having alternative cultural preferences, many went to the "wrong" countries. The south-south flows from Italy, Spain, and Portugal to Brazil and Argentina were a strong force for local (Latin) convergence, but not global convergence. Furthermore, while barriers to exit were virtually absent in most of the Old World, policy (like assisted passage) still played a part in violating any simple market-wage calculus.[8] However, the small contribution of migration to convergence within the Old World and within the New illustrates my opening point: the major contribution of mass migration to late nineteenth-century convergence was the enormous movement of 50 or 60 million Europeans to the New World.

The relative insensitivity of GDP per capita convergence to migration is a result of countervailing economic forces. For real wages or GDP per worker, high migrant-to-population ratios of labor participation rates amplify the impact of migration, but with GDP per capita the impact is muted. Why? In the former two cases, migration has a bigger impact on the labor force, GDP, and wages, the bigger is the labor content of the migrations. In the case of GDP per capita, things are less clear. For example, with emigration, population outflow generally offsets diminishing returns in production for a net positive impact on output per capita; but selectivity assures that emigration will take away a disproportionate share of the labor force, lowering output via labor supply losses, a negative impact on output per capita. The latter effect dominated in the late nineteenth-century Atlantic

---

[8] Barriers to exit did exist in countries outside my Atlantic economy sample: for example, most emigration from Russia was illegal.

economy, so muted GDP per capita effects are no surprise. Based on table 2.3, four decades of migration never lowered GDP per capita by more than 9 percent anywhere in the New World, and by as little as 3 percent in the United States, in contrast with per worker impacts of 27 and 9 percent, respectively. This labor-supply compensation effect operated in addition to the usual human-capital transfer influences invoked to describe the net benefit to the United States of the millions received before World War I (Neal and Uselding 1972). Similar reasoning applies to the Old World: Swedish emigration after 1870 may have raised wages in 1910 by about 9 percent but it served to raise GDP per capita by only 2 percent.

2.10 Qualifying the assessment of the globalization impact

I have argued that mass migration might have accounted for 125 percent of the real wage convergence observed in the Atlantic economy between 1870 and 1910. Have I overexplained late nineteenth-century convergence? Perhaps, but remember that there were *other* powerful pro-convergence and anti-convergence forces at work. Consider capital accumulation. We know that capital accumulation was faster in the New World, so much so that the rate of capital deepening was faster in the United States than in any of her competitors (Wright 1990; Wolff 1991), and the same was probably true of other rich New World countries. There is ample evidence therefore that the mass migrations may have been at least partially offset by capital accumulation, and a large part of that capital widening was being carried by international capital flows which reached magnitudes unsurpassed before or since (Edelstein 1982; Zevin 1992; Taylor 1996). The evidence on the role of global capital-market responses to migration is very tentative (O'Rourke and Williamson 1997a: chapter 11), but Alan Taylor and I make a rough adjustment along these lines to the results reported in table 2.3. They implement the zero-net-migration counterfactual in a model where the labor supply shocks generate capital inflows or outflows in order to maintain a constant rate of return to capital in each country.[9] The capital-chasing-labor offsets are very large. Whereas mass migration over explained 125 percent of the observed real wage convergence using the model without capital chasing labor, it explains about 40 percent of the convergence using the model with capital chasing labor.

Earlier in this chapter, I reported research that suggested that perhaps 10 percent of the real wage and living standard convergence might have been explained by trade. Now it appears that mass migration, properly adjusted for capital chasing after labor, might account for another 40 percent. Thus, globalization through trade and factor flows probably accounted for half of the real wage and living standard convergence before 1914, leaving the other half for other forces. The forces of late nineteenth-century convergence included commodity price convergence and trade expansion, technological catch-up, and human-capital accumulation, but mass migration was clearly the central force. Capital flows were mainly an anti-convergence force (Scandinavia being an outstanding exception), in that they raised wages and labor productivity in the labor-scarce and resource-abundant New World.[10]

These results offer a new perspective on the convergence debate. The indirect influence of trade on convergence was modest in the half century prior to 1914. In contrast, free migration had a powerful and direct impact on the convergence of real wages and living standards across countries. Late nineteenth-century convergence explanations based on technological catch-up and accumulation in closed-economy models miss this point. The millions on the move prior to 1914 did not.

---

[9] This extreme capital-chasing assumption does not imply that capital-labor ratios are everywhere the same, or even that they return to levels held prior to the mass migration shocks. After all, there is a third factor, resources, in the model, and thus even identical capital-labor ratios would not imply identical wages and living standards.

[10] In 1990, Robert Lucas published an article which asked why far more capital did not flow from rich to poor countries in the 1980s. The same can be said about the 1880s. The vast majority of the capital leaving Britain flowed to the resource abundant New World where labor was scarce. A very small share of it went to poor labor abundant countries. A third factor, natural resources, was pulling both capital and labor from Europe to the New World.

THREE

Policy backlash: can the past inform the present?

3.1 Can the past inform the present?

It turns out that the late nineteenth and the late twentieth century shared more than simply globalization and convergence. Globalization also had the same impact on income distribution: inequality rose in rich countries and fell in poor countries; though much debated, some think the same trends are apparent now. And while globalization, according to some, accounted for about a third to a half of the rise in inequality in America and other OECD countries since the 1970s, it probably accounted for more in the late nineteenth century. It also appears that the inequality which globalization produced prior to World War I was partly responsible for the interwar retreat from globalization. What is in store for the future? Will the world economy retreat once again from globalization as these inequality side effects in the rich OECD have their political impact?

As we have seen, there were three epochs of growth experience after the mid nineteenth century for what is now called the OECD:

This lecture draws heavily on my own previous work (Williamson 1996, 1997a, 1997b), and that in collaboration with Kevin O'Rourke (O'Rourke and Williamson 1997a) and Ashley Timmer (1997). I gratefully acknowledge the collaboration with these two colleagues, and their generous permission to allow me to draw on our joint work for this lecture.

the late nineteenth-century *belle epoque*, the dark middle ages between 1914 and 1950, and the late twentieth-century renaissance. The first and last epochs were ones of overall fast growth, convergence (poor countries catching up on rich), and globalization (trade booms, mass migration and huge capital flows). The middle ages were ones of overall slow growth, de-globalization, and divergence. Thus, history offers an unambiguous positive correlation between globalization and convergence. When the pre-World War I years are examined in detail, the correlation turns out to be causal: the last chapter argued that globalization served to play *the* critical role in contributing to convergence; it took the form of mass migration and trade.

Since contemporary economists are now hotly debating the impact of these globalization forces on wage inequality in the OECD, the Latin American recently liberal regimes, and the open Asian tigers, it seems timely to ask whether the same distributional forces were at work during the late nineteenth century. There is a literature a century old which argues that immigration hurt American labor and accounted for much of the rise in inequality from the 1890s to World War I, so much so that a labor-sympathetic Congress passed immigration quotas. There is a literature even older which argues that the New World grain invasion eroded land rents in Europe, so much so that landowner-dominated continental parliaments raised tariffs to help protect them from the impact of globalization. But nowhere in this historical literature has anyone constructed a panel data set across countries and over time – like Adrian Wood (1994) has done recently for the late twentieth century – which could be used to test three contentious hypotheses with important policy implications:

> **Hypothesis 1** Inequality rose in resource-rich, labor-scarce New World countries like Argentina, Australia, Canada, and, most importantly, the United States. Inequality fell in resource-poor, labor-abundant, agrarian countries around the European periphery like Italy, the Iberian Peninsula, Ireland, and Scandinavia. Inequality was more stable for the European industrial leaders like Britain,

France, Germany, and the Lowlands all of whom fell
somewhere in the middle between the rich New World
and poor Europe.

Hypothesis 2 If the first hypothesis survives test, then a
second follows: these inequality patterns can be
explained largely by globalization.

Hypothesis 3 If the second hypothesis survives testing, then
a third follows: these globalization-induced inequality
trends help explain the retreat from globalization during
the dark ages between 1914 and 1950.

This last chapter begins by reviewing the theory and comparing
the historical debate about the first globalization boom in the late
nineteenth century with current debate about the second globalization boom in the late twentieth century. There is a striking sim-
ilarity between the two debates. There is also a shared
short-coming to the empirical analysis: nobody has yet explored
this issue with late nineteenth-century panel data across poor
and rich countries, and, with the important exception of Adrian
Wood (1994), few have done so for the late twentieth-century
debate either. Indeed, until very recently, most economists had
focused solely on the American experience. The lecture reports a
late nineteenth-century database which includes both rich and
poor countries, or, in the modern vernacular, north and south. It
then shows how this new database has been used to establish the
late nineteenth-century facts: **Hypothesis 1** survives. **Hypothesis
2** also survives, but it looks like it was international migration
rather than trade that mattered most.

It appears that globalization did drive inequality before the
interwar age of autarky. That fact seems to offer support for
Hypothesis 3, namely, it contributed to the implosion, de-globalization, and autarkic policies which dominated between 1914 and
1950. Indeed, during this dark age of trade suppression and
binding migration quotas, the old globalization–distribution
connection completely disappeared. It took the globalization
renaissance after the early 1970s to renew this old inequality
debate. However, there were strong forces already at work which
were rejecting trade and migration liberalization or openness

before World War I. The lecture shows the strong connections between the pre-1914 distribution trends and a policy backlash to globalization.

3.2 Globalization and inequality: the late twentieth-century debate

After 1973 and especially in the 1980s, the United States experienced a dismal real wage performance for the less skilled, mostly due to declining productivity growth coupled with increasing wage inequality between skills. The ratio of weekly wages of the top decile to the lowest decile increased from 2.9 in 1963 to 4.4 in 1989 (Kosters 1994; Freeman 1995). This inequality was manifested primarily by increasing wage premia for workers with advanced schooling and age-related skills. While the same inequality trends were apparent elsewhere in the OECD in the 1980s, the increase was typically far smaller (Kosters 1994). Most of the current debate has focused on explaining these inequality facts. These inequality developments coincided with globalization, both in the form of rising trade and immigration. The latter has taken the form of rising rates of US immigration and a decline in its "quality" (Borjas 1994). US trade shares increased from 12 percent of GNP in 1970 to 25 percent in 1990 (Lawrence and Slaughter 1993), while World Bank figures document that the share of output exported from low-income countries rose from 8 percent in 1965 to 18 percent in 1990 (Richardson 1995: 34). These inequality developments also coincided with a shift in US spending patterns which resulted in large trade deficits. Thus, economists have quite naturally explored the linkages between trade and immigration, on the one hand, and wage inequality, on the other.

The standard Heckscher–Ohlin trade model makes unambiguous predictions. Every country exports those products which use intensively abundant and cheap factors of production. Thus, a trade boom induced by either declining tariffs or transport costs will cause exports and the demand for the cheap factor to boom too. Globalization in poor countries should favor unskilled labor and dis-favor skilled labor; globalization in rich countries should favor skilled labor and dis-favor unskilled labor. Robert Lawrence and Matthew Slaughter (1993) used the standard Heckscher–Ohlin model to explore recent wage inequality and concluded that there is little evidence to support it. Instead, the authors concluded that technological change was an important source of rising wage inequality since the 1970s. Hot debate ensued, with no resolution in sight.

This strand of the debate stressed the evolution of labor demand by skill, ignoring the potential influence of supply. George Borjas (1994) and his collaborators (Borjas, Freeman, and Katz 1992) took a different approach, emphasizing instead how trade and immigration served to augment US labor supply. In order to do this, they first estimate the implicit labor supply embodied in trade flows. Imports embody labor thus serving to augment effective domestic labor supply. Likewise, exports imply a decrease in the effective domestic labor supply. In this way, the huge US trade deficit of the 1980s implied a 1.5 percent increase in the US labor supply and, since most of the imports were in goods which used unskilled labor relatively intensively, it also implied an increasing ratio of unskilled to skilled effective labor supplies. In addition, there was a shift in national origin of immigrants from the 1960s to the 1980s so that an increasing proportion of immigrants were from the less-developed nations (e.g., Mexico and Asia) and thus more unskilled, which in turn meant a far higher fraction of immigrants were relatively unskilled just when there were more of them. It follows that both trade and immigration increased the supply of unskilled relative to skilled workers in the 1980s.

These relative supply shifts give us the desired qualitative result – wage inequality between skill types. The quantitative result, at least in Borjas' hands, also seems big. Borjas estimates that 15–25 percent of the relative wage decline of high school to college graduates is due to trade and immigration. He also estimates that 30–50 percent of the decline in relative wage of high school dropouts to all other workers is due to these same globalization forces, one-third of which was due to trade and two-thirds to immigration. Migration was the more important globalization force producing US inequality trends in the 1980s according to Borjas. We shall see in a moment that it was *far* more important in the late nineteenth century, and, furthermore, that it was ubiquitous across practically all countries involved in the globalization experience.

Thus far, I have been talking about only one country, the United States, perhaps because this is where rising inequality and immigration have been greatest. But the question is not simply why the United States and even Europe experienced a depressed relative demand for low-skilled labor in the 1980s and 1990s (Freeman 1995: 19), but whether the same factors were *stimulating* the relative demand for low-skill labor in the poor Third World. This is where Adrian Wood (1994, chapter 6; 1995b) enters the debate. Wood was one of the first economists to examine systematically inequality trends across countries, *including* the poor south.

Wood distinguishes three skill types: uneducated, labor with basic education and the highly educated. The poor south is richly endowed with uneducated labor but the supply of labor with basic skills is growing fast. The rich north is, of course, abundant in highly educated labor with a slow growing supply of labor with basic skills. Wood assumes capital is fairly mobile and that technology is freely available. As the south improves its skills through the expansion of basic education and trade barriers fall, it produces more manufactures that require only basic skills whereas the north produces more of the high-skill goods. It follows that the ratio of the unskilled to the skilled wage should rise in the south and fall in the north. The tendency toward relative factor price convergence raises the relative wage of workers with a basic education in the south and lowers it in the north, producing, *ceteris paribus*, rising inequality in the north and falling inequality in the south.

Basing his results on insights derived from classical Heckscher–Ohlin theory (extended by Stolper–Samuelson), Wood concludes that the decline in the relative wage of less-skilled northern workers is due to the elimination of trade barriers and increasing relative abundance of southern workers with a basic education. He also dismisses biased technological change as a potential explanation since labor and total factor productivity growth both slowed down during the period when inequality was rising. Wood also argues that the pattern of increasing wage inequality in the north favors a trade explanation since there is no cross-country association between inequality trends and technological progress rates.

Wood's research has been met with stiff critical resistance. Since his book appeared, we have learned more about the inequality and globalization connection in the Third World. The standard Stolper–Samuelson prediction would be that unskilled-labor-abundant poor countries should undergo egalitarian trends in the face of globalization forces, unless they are overwhelmed by inequality forces like: industrial revolutionary labor-saving events on the upswing of the Kuznets Curve – early industrialization where Kuznets (1955) hypothesized rising inequality, and/or Mathusian gluts generated by the demographic transition – early industrialization where falling infant mortality generates a rapid growth in new labor force entrants 15–20 years later, glutting the bottom of the income pyramid where the impecunious young typically reside (Bloom and Williamson 1996, 1997); and/or a shortfall in schooling supplies which raises the premium on scarce skills (Williamson 1993). A recent review by Donald Davis (1996) reports no such egalitarian trends, and a study of seven countries in Latin America and East Asia shows that wage inequality typically did not fall after trade liberalization, but rather *rose* (Robbins 1996). This apparent anomaly has been strengthened by other studies, some of which have been rediscovered since Wood's book appeared. For example, almost twenty years ago Anne Krueger (1978) studied ten developing countries covering the period through 1972, and her findings were not favorable to the simple predictions of standard trade theory. Her conclusions have been supported by Bourguignon and Morrisson (1991), and by recent work on the impact of Mexican liberalization on wage inequality (Feenstra and Hanson 1995; Feliciano 1995). Of course, none of these studies are very attentive to the simultaneous role of emigration from these developing countries.

The debate on the late twentieth-century globalization and inequality connection is far from resolved. Perhaps some fresh evidence from an earlier globalization experience might help us find a resolution.

3.3 Globalization and inequality: the late nineteenth-century debate

Lecture two showed that the late nineteenth century was a period of dramatic commodity market integration: railways and steamships lowered transport costs, and Europe moved toward free trade in the wake of the 1860 Cobden-Chevalier treaty. These developments implied large trade-creating price shocks which affected every European participant, the cannonical case being the drop in European grain prices. Furthermore, it applied to all tradeables, not just grain. These globalization price shocks were considerably bigger than those implied by the GATT-induced decline in OECD tariff barriers in the three decades following the 1940s, policy events which triggered the globalization boom we have witnessed over the last quarter century. To repeat, the World Bank reports that tariffs on manufactures entering developed countries fell from 40 percent in the late 1940s to 7 percent in the late 1970s, for a thirty year fall of 33 percentage points (about eight-tenths of the original 40 percent in the late 1940s). Wood (1994: 173) uses this example to advertize just how revolutionary world commodity-market integration has been in the late twentieth century, but this spectacular post-war reclamation of free trade from interwar autarky was actually smaller than the 45 percentage point fall in trade barriers between 1870 and 1913 due to transport improvements. In addition, policy did not contribute to increased globalization between 1870 and World War I since the period was one of liberal retreat and higher tariffs in the Atlantic economy.

Eli Heckscher and Bertil Ohlin argued that such commodity-market integration should have led to international factor price convergence, as countries everywhere expanded the production and export of commodities which used their abundant (and cheap) factors relatively intensively. Thus, the late nineteenth-century trade boom accounted for perhaps 10–20 percent of the convergence in GDP per worker hour and in the real wage. It had bigger distributional implications. For poor labor-abundant and land-scarce countries, it meant rising unskilled wages relative to rents and skilled wages. For rich labor-scarce and land-abundant countries, it meant falling unskilled wages relative to rents and skilled wages.

What about mass migration? The correlation between real wages or GDP per worker hour and migration rates is positive and highly significant. The poorest Old World countries tended to have the highest emigration rates while the richest New World countries tended to have the highest immigration rates. The correlation is not perfect since potential emigrants from poor countries often found the cost of the move too high, and some New World countries restricted the inflow of those from the poor European periphery. But the correlation is still very strong. Furthermore, the average labor force impact was very big, much bigger than US experience in the 1980s: it augmented the New World labor force by about 40 percent and reduced the Old World labor force by 18 percent, at least among the emigrant countries around the European periphery. In any case, the conclusion of lecture two estimated that the mass migrations explain at least 40 percent of the real wage convergence in the late nineteenth century. Note that this estimate, in contrast with contemporary debate about the United States in the 1980s, includes the total impact on both *rich* receiving countries and *poor* sending countries.

Since the migrants tended to be unskilled and increasingly so as the late nineteenth century unfolded (much like the late twentieth century), they served to flood the immigrant country labor markets at the bottom, thus lowering the unskilled wage relative to the skilled wage, white-collar income and land rents. Immigration implied rising inequality in labor-scrace, resource-rich countries. Emigration implied falling inequality in labor abundant, resource poor countries.

So much for plausible assertions. What were the facts?

3.4 Globalization and inequality: the historical facts

The inequality facts, 1870–1913

Complete income distributions at various benchmarks between the mid nineteenth century and World War II are unavailable except for a few countries and dates, but even if they were it is not obvious that we would want them to test the impact of globalization. Like economists involved in the modern debate, our interest here is factor prices: unskilled wages, skilled wages, land rents and profit rates. How did the typical unskilled worker near the bottom of the distribution do relative to the typical landowner or capitalist near the top, or even relative to the typical skilled blue-collar worker or educated white-collar employee near the middle of the distribution? Modern debate has a fixation on wage inequality, but since land and landed interests were far more important to late nineteenth-century inequality trends, we need to add them to our distribution inquiry.[1] In any case, we have two kinds of evidence available to document late nineteenth-century inequality trends so defined: the ratio of the unskilled wage to farm rents per acre, and the ratio of the unskilled wage to GDP per worker.

Recall from table 1.2 that relative factor price convergence *did* characterize the four decades prior to World War I. The wage–rental ratio plunged in the New World, where it had been initially high. The Australian ratio had fallen to one-quarter of its 1870 level by 1913, the Argentine ratio had fallen to one-fifth of its mid 1880 level, and the US ratio had fallen to less than half of its 1870 level. In Europe, the (initially low) wage–rental ratio surged up to World War I. The British ratio increased by a factor of 2.7 over its 1870 level, while the Irish ratio increased by even more. The Swedish and Danish ratios both increased by a factor of 2.3. Not surprisingly, the surge was more pronounced in free-trade than in protectionist countries. As prime examples of the latter, the ratio increased "only" by a factor of 1.8 in France, 1.4 in Germany, and not at all in Spain.

Since landowners tended to be near the top of the distribution,[2]

---

[1] Recent studies of the Third World globalization–inequality connection also tend to focus on wage inequality, and sometimes even only *urban* wage inequality. This is a big mistake for countries where rural wage employment is important and where landed interests are powerful. The economic position of the landlord and the rural laborer matter in economies where agriculture is a fifth, a quarter, or even a third of the economy.

[2] This was certainly true of Europe, Argentina, and the American South, but less true for the American Midwest and Canada where the family farm dominated.

this evidence is consistent with the hypothesis that inequality rose in the rich, labor-scarce New World, while inequality fell in poor, labor-abundant Europe. There is also some evidence that globalization mattered: European countries staying open absorbed the biggest distributional hit; European countries retreating behind tariff walls absorbed the smallest distributional hit (Williamson 1997a).

So much for wage–rental ratios. What about the ratio of the unskilled worker's wage (w) to the returns on all factors per laborer, namely Maddison's (1995) GDP per worker estimates (y)? Changes in the ratio w/y measure changes in the economic distance between the working poor near the bottom of the distribution and the average working adult in the middle of the distribution. It turns out that this simple statistic is highly correlated with more comprehensive inequality measures during the interwar years when full income distribution data are far more abundant (Williamson 1997a).

The fourteen countries in our sample exhibited *very* different inequality trends. When the index is normalized by setting w/y equal to 100 in 1870, we get the following: powerful Danish and Swedish equality trends establish the upper bound (the index rises to about 153 or 154); and powerful Australian and United States inequality trends establish the lower bound (the index falls to about 53 or 58). An alternative way to standardize these distributional trends is to compute the annual percentage change in the index relative to its 1870 base: the per annum rates range from + 0.97 and + 0.98 for Denmark and Sweden respectively, to − 1.22 and − 1.45 for Australia and the United States respectively. This measure of inequality change is plotted against the 1870 real wage in figure 3.1, and it offers a stunning confirmation of the globalization hypothesis: between 1870 and 1913 inequality rose dramatically in rich, labor-scarce New World countries like Australia, Canada, and the United States; inequality fell dramatically in poor, labor-abundant, newly industrializing countries like Norway, Sweden, Denmark, and Italy; inequality was more stable in the European industrial economies like Belgium, France, Germany, The Netherlands, and the United Kingdom; and inequality was also more stable in the poor European economies

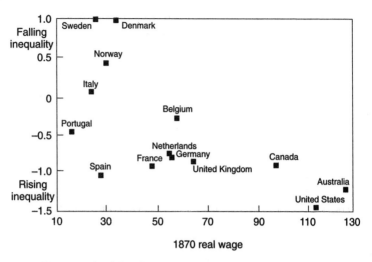

Figure 3.1 Initial real wages versus inequality trends, 1870–1913
Source: Williamson (1997a, figure 4).

which failed to play the globalization game, like Portugal and Spain.

The correlation in figure 3.1 is really quite amazing given the state of the literature on the Kuznets Curve. When Kuznets made his presidential address to the American Economic Association in 1955, he hypothesized that inequality should rise in the early stages of modern development, reach a peak during what we have come to call the NIC (newly industrialized country) stage, and then fall thereafter. Montek Ahluwalia (1976) and his World Bank colleagues offered two decades of post-World War II evidence that seemed to confirm the Kuznets Curve. Since then, the thesis has taken a beating, most recently with late twentieth-century data by Klaus Deiniger and Lyn Squire (1996). What is surprising about this literature, however, is that it treats a very complex problem so simply. There are a number of forces that can drive inequality in the long run, and I listed some of them above. To repeat, they are: globalization, demography, schooling, and technology. It appears that one of these forces, globalization, is doing most of the work in the late nineteenth-century Atlantic economy. This can be seen clearly in figure 3.2 where the impact of mass migration on labor

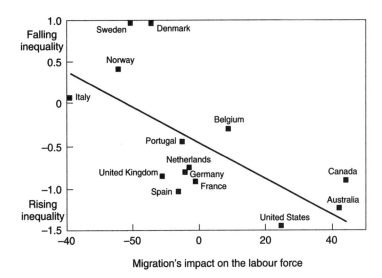

Figure 3.2 Inequality trends versus migration's impact on the labor force, 1870–1913
Source: Williamson (1997a, figure 5).

supplies (table 2.1) is plotted against the inequality evidence: where immigration increased the receiving country's labor supply greatly, inequality rose sharply; where emigration reduced the sending country's labor supply markedly, inequality declined. In addition, explicit multivariate econometric analysis offers very strong support for the view that mass migration had a powerful influence on income distribution but only weak support for the view that trade mattered.

The inequality facts, 1921–1938

Did citizens living through these events feel that globalization accounted for these distributional trends? Did they modify their open and liberal policies in response? Did the policy switch matter? The remainder of this chapter will establish the globalization backlash connection, but it might be useful to see whether inequality trends changed during the interwar period when

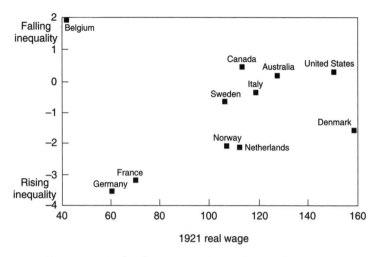

Figure 3.3 Initial real wage versus inequality trends, 1921–1938
Source: Williamson (1997a, figure 6).

quotas were imposed in immigrating countries, when capital markets collapsed in the face of government intervention, and when trade barriers soared to autarkic heights – that is, under conditions of de-globalization.

First, and to repeat a key finding of the first lecture, convergence ceased. Figure 1.4 documents divergence for real wages between 1914 and 1937. Some of the divergence was war related, and some of it was great depression related, but even during the 1920s, convergence ceased.

Second, the globalization–inequality connection was broken. Figure 3.3 shows the correlation between 1921 and 1938 inequality trends as measured by changes in w/y and a 1921 real wage measure of labor scarcity. The late nineteenth-century inverse correlation has completely disappeared, replaced by a positive correlation. In the interwar period of de-globalization, the poorer countries underwent sharply increasing inequality while the richer countries underwent more moderate increases, or, in four cases, egalitarian trends. Is this correlation between distribution trends and globalization commitments in the Atlantic economy spurious? Contemporary observers did not think so.

The interwar egalitarian trends in the United States do not

begin until after 1929, and they were sufficiently dramatic that one observer called it "revolutionary" (Burns 1954). It seems surprising that the literature has spent so little time exploring the extent to which the disappearance of mass migration and the collapse of world trade might explain a good share of that revolution.

3.5 Globalization backlash: immigration restrictions

Measuring immigration policy

The American doors did not suddenly and without warning slam shut on European emigrants when the United States Congress overrode President Wilson's veto of the immigrant literacy test in February 1917 or when it passed the Emergency Quota Act of May 1921. Over the half-century prior to the Literacy Act, the United States had been imposing restrictions on what had been free immigration (e.g., contract labor laws, Asian exclusion acts, excludable classes, head taxes, policies that discriminated against the recent foreign-born and favored the native-born, and so on), and had long been debating more severe restrictions. The Quota Act of 1921 was preceded by a quarter century of active Congressional debate, and the first vote in 1897 had 86 percent of the Congressmen opting for more restriction (e.g., the literacy requirement: Goldin 1994: table 7.1). And the United States was hardly alone. Argentina, Australia, Brazil, and Canada enacted similar measures, although the timing was sometimes different, and the policies more often took the form of an enormous drop in or even disappearance of large immigrant subsidies rather than of outright exclusion. Contrary to the conventional wisdom, therefore, it was not simply one big regime switch around World War I from free immigration to quotas, but rather an evolution towards a less generous and more restrictive immigration policy. To ignore this fact is to miss important evidence of globalization backlash in the past.

How do we construct an index which can quantify immigration policy? Such an index could then be used to assess the extent to which globalization backlash was at work and, if so, to identify the form that it took. Two recent papers designed and implemented a policy index which ranges over a scale of $+5$ to -5 (Timmer and Williamson 1996, 1997).[3] A positive score denotes a pro-immigration policy, typically including comprehensive subsidies for passage and support upon arrival. A negative score denotes anti-immigration policy, typically an outright ban on some groups, quotas, head taxes, literacy tests, and discriminatory treatment upon arrival. A zero denotes policy neutrality.

The policy indices (POLICY) plotted in figure 3.4 are quite clear regarding the very long run. Despite universal openness to immigration in the 1860s, the New World doors were effectively closed by 1930. Argentina's index dropped from $+4.5$ in the late 1880s to -2.5 in the mid 1920s, a 7 point fall (out of a possible 10). Brazil's index underwent a similar decline, although it all came in a rush at the end of the period. Australia's index fell from $+3$ in the mid 1860s to -2 in 1930, for a 5 point fall. The index for the United States fell from 0 in the early 1860s to -5 by the 1930, a 5 point fall. Canada's index fell from $+2$ in the mid 1870s to -4.5 by 1920, a 6.5 point fall. The policy evolution varied widely over those seven decades: Argentina and the United States exhibited a steady drift away from free immigration; Brazil remained open much longer, suddenly slamming the door shut in the 1920s; and Canada reversed the trend in the 1920s while Australia did it more than once over the period.

Although there are some cases of remarkable short-term variance, strong persistence is more notable. Policy was slow to change, sometimes constant over a decade or more, even though there was almost always intensive political debate underlying that apparent quiescence. The best examples of this stability are Brazil over the three decades from 1890 to 1920, a period which ended in 1921 when subsidies disappeared and tough immigration restrictions were imposed, and the United States from 1888 to 1916, a period which produced intense debate, the famous 1911 Immigration Commission Report

[3] It takes some doing to summarize these policies with a score for each year, but applied economists struggle with the same problem when trying to summarize just how open a country's trade policy is at any point in time (Anderson and Neary 1994; Sachs and Warner 1995a).

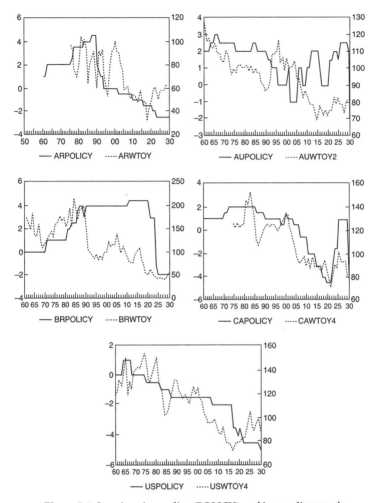

Figure 3.4 Immigration policy (POLICY) and inequality trends (WTOY) prior to the 1930s
Source: Timmer and Williamson (1997, figure 2, revised).

(which strongly recommended restriction), the successful congressional override of President Wilson's veto in 1917, and finally the quotas in 1921. Given that policy was often slow to change, it is important not to confuse short-run influences on the timing of policy change with the long-run fundamentals underlying the evolution of policy.

Immigration policy: searching for hypotheses

There is a general consensus in the historical literature that immigration policy has always been sensitive to labor-market conditions. At the same time, immigration flows themselves have always been sensitive to real wage and unemployment rate differentials. We know, for example, that there was a strong push for immigration restrictions in the United States in the late 1890s, a time of economic recession and high unemployment. The rate of immigration slowed dramatically at that time, however, reaching a secular low in 1897, the same year that the first vote on immigration restriction was taken in the House of Representatives. Similarly, Australian inflows dropped sharply in the recession of the 1890s when attitudes toward immigrant subsidies hardened. These events suggest that immigration restrictions rarely appeared when immigration flows were big. On the contrary, when immigration rates dropped to a trickle during each slump, governments would typically use immigration restrictions as a politically safe policy to ease unemployment. Such "guestworker policy" reactions were not only ineffective but unnecessary during an era when safety-nets for new immigrants were non-existent; the return migration rate was enormous during slumps, and during the big slumps of the 1870s and 1890s, the United States recorded net emigration rates (Hatton and Williamson 1997: chapter 8).

Policies to restrict immigration were far more sensitive to labor-market conditions than they were to the sheer size of the immigration flows. Inequality is one manifestation of these labor-market conditions, and the living standards of the working poor is another. Both figured prominently in the debate.

How should immigration policy respond to rising inequality or to deteriorating living standards for the workers? Do rational and farsighted voters consider the impact of immigration on future economic growth? If so, how would they assess it? Immigration induces falling wages and greater inequality, but does rising inequality augment or inhibit economic growth? The traditional Smithian view had it that the rising inequality would place relatively more income in the hands of those who save, thus raising the investment rate and growth. Modern political economists take a different view, arguing that if a country lets its poorest voters become too poor, richer voters might join poorer voters to pass distortionary redistributive policies that can slow growth (Alesina and Perotti 1994; Perotti 1996). Economists do not yet have a clear answer to this question, especially for a century ago when government redistributive intervention was modest. But citizens may vote for immigration restriction for other reasons: they may simply dislike the increased blight inequality creates and the deterioration in their unskilled neighbors' living standards; and they may fear that these events may provoke some political rebellion from below. Furthermore, since unskilled labor had a stronger political voice in the labor-scarce immigration countries, their economic condition was more likely to be translated into a restrictive policy response.

Immigration policy: some evidence

The empirical literature on the determinants of immigration policy is very new, so that much of what follows is still speculative. But some outlines are beginning to emerge (Timmer and Williamson 1996, 1997).

The most consistent effect is that immigration policy was slow to change. This was especially true of Brazil and the United States even after controlling for all the variables that seem to have influenced policy. But it is worth noting that these two countries with the strongest historical persistence also exhibit the biggest policy switch at the end of their periods of quiescence, from wide open to tightly closed. Big policy switches usually required long periods of debate. Persistence offers more evidence in support of the view that current macroeconomic conditions – like unemployment rates – are unlikely to help account for long-run policy changes regarding immigration.

Labor-market conditions also had a consistent influence on immigration policy, and it appears that both the absolute and relative income performance of unskilled workers mattered. The econometrics suggests that poor wage performance was associated with more restrictive policy in Australia, Brazil, and the United

States. However, the most consistently significant variable reported by Timmer and Williamson is w/y, the ratio of the unskilled wage to income per worker, or of income near the bottom of the distribution to income in the middle. Rising inequality was associated with increasingly restrictive immigration policy. It is well known that (new) immigrants were unskilled and tended to cluster at the bottom of the distribution, at least initially, and that this was increasingly true as the late nineteenth century unfolded. Regardless of what else is included in the regression, this measure of unskilled labor's relative economic performance stands out as an important influence on policy. Rising relative unskilled labor scarcity encouraged more open immigration policies; declining relative unskilled labor scarcity encouraged more restrictive immigration policies.[4] The correlation is apparent in figure 3.4.

The evidence just summarized speaks to the indirect impact of immigration on policy by looking at absolute and relative wage performance in labor-markets. What about the direct impact of immigration on policy? Perhaps the size and character of the current and expected future immigrant flow precipitated policy change, the latter serving to anticipate the labor market impact. Two variables might serve to measure these direct immigration effects. First, one might use some proxy for the quality, or human-capital content, of the immigrants and the change in that quality proxy.[5] Second, one might measure immigrant quantity by the foreign-born population share. However measured, low and falling immigrant quality precipitated more restrictive immigrant policy, even after controlling for other forces. To some extent, therefore, New World policy anticipated the impact of low-quality immigrants on unskilled wages and moved to shut it down. Ethnic attributes of the immigrants – differences in ethnic composition between the current immigration flow and the foreign population stock – seem to have had little bearing on policy. Feelings about race and ethnicity do not matter much to policy choices after one controls for labor market influences. Increasing racism, xenopho-

---

[4] Furthermore, this effect is likely to be biased downwards since open immigration policy implies more immigrants and lower w/y, as I argued above.
[5] One such proxy that has been effective is the real wage of unskilled urban workers in the source countries.

bia, and widening ethnicity gaps between current and previous immigration may have reached the popular press, but they did not have a big impact on voting behavior.

To what extent was a change in a country's policy in part a reaction to changes in immigration policy elsewhere? As expected, the United States – the New World immigrant leader – was completely unresponsive to competitors' policies. For most other countries, policy elsewhere mattered a great deal. For Argentina, it was the combined impact of Australian, Canadian, and Brazilian policy that mattered, more restrictive policy abroad inducing more restrictive policy at home. Brazil tended to mimic the policies followed by Argentina and the United States. Australia tended to favor open immigration policies when the United Kingdom offered more generous subsidies to its emigrants, and also, to some extent, when Canada adopted more open policies.

To summarize, while the size of the immigrant flow did not seem to have any consistent impact on New World policy up to 1930, its low and declining quality certainly did, provoking restriction. Policies adopted by one's competitors mattered even more. Labor-market conditions mattered most, deteriorating conditions provoking a restrictive policy reaction. The labor-scarce New World acted to defend the economic interests of unskilled labor toward the bottom of the distribution pyramid.

3.6 Globalization backlash: European tariffs

The end of a liberal interlude

Land-abundant New World economies became increasingly integrated with labor-abundant European economies in the late nineteenth century. While the distributional impact of this shock varied from country to country, there is broad support for the Heckscher–Ohlin prediction that European land and American labor suffered. Not surprisingly, European agricultural interests lobbied for protection. Landowners were successful in some countries, such as France and Germany, and tariffs were introduced. These tariffs can be viewed as the precursors of today's European Common Agricultural Policy. Other countries, like Britain, Ireland, and Denmark, stuck to their free trade guns, forcing agriculture to adapt or decline.

What explains the differing European political responses to the grain invasion? While this question has become canonical in the comparative political economy literature, only recently has it been decomposed into the relevant component parts: the size of the globalization shock, it's distributional impact, and, only then, the policy response (O'Rourke 1997a; O'Rourke and Williamson 1997a: chapter 5). The traditional literature typically deals with the policy response only.

The impact of protection on domestic markets

Were late nineteenth-century tariffs high enough to matter? Did they really impede the integration of international commodity markets, or was their impact swamped by the steep decline in transport costs which generated the tariff response in the first place? Did they only serve to signal that a more severe interwar globalization backlash was yet to come?

Since agricultural interests were getting hit hardest, the best place to seek the answers to these questions is by looking at domestic grain markets. Tariffs certainly raised domestic prices, but the issue is whether they raised them enough to insulate continental Europe from the globalizing impact of steamships, railroads, and international canals. It appears that they did. German grain prices did not converge on American prices at all, French and Swedish prices converged only modestly, and British and Danish prices converged dramatically. The contrast between free-trading Europe (Britain and Denmark) and protectionist Europe (Germany, France, and Sweden) is also born out when European prices are compared with those of the Ukraine. In short, there is absolutely no evidence of grain-market integration on the continent during the forty years prior to World War I. An era when Europe and New World became globally integrated was also one when grain markets *within* Europe became more balkanized. Globalization was not a universal phenomenon, even during the comparatively liberal late nineteenth century. Tariff hikes were big enough to mattter.

Distributional impact and policy backlash

The contributions of Charles Kindleberger (1951) and Ronald Rogowski (1989) stand out in this literature which seeks to explain tariff responses to grain invasions. Oddly enough, Rogowski the political scientist uses a conventional Heckscher–Ohlin model to sort the problem out, while Kindleberger the economist uses sociology and political science. Yet, both authors implicitly assume that the grain invasion generated the same shock to all economies, and that identical price shocks had the same impact on income distribution. Neither assumption held, as Kevin O'Rourke (1997a) has recently shown, and as I pointed out in the previous chapter. It might be useful to repeat those findings.

Consider the first assumption. Denmark was a free trader, but experienced a far more modest farm price shock than did Britain. While real cereal prices fell by 29 percent in Britain between 1870 and 1913, they fell by only 10 percent in Denmark. Without protection, French and German cereal prices would have declined by 34 percent under free trade, and Swedish prices would have declined by 27 percent. If the grain invasion lowered cereal prices by less in Denmark than in the rest of Europe, then the grain invasion lowered Danish rents by less as well. O'Rourke estimates the elasticity of land prices with respect to grain prices at around 0.5. The elasticity implies that the cost to French, German, and Swedish landowners of maintaining free trade in the face of the grain invasion was a 12 to 18 percent reduction in land values, while cheap grain lowered Danish land values by only 4 or 5 percent. Moreover, globalization raised the prices of Danish animal products exported to British markets. Armed with this new evidence, the Danish decision not to protect agriculture seems less surprising.

Second, even identical price shocks can have very different effects on income distribution, depending on the structure of production. Agriculture was relatively small in Britain, an industrial leader. Britain was also more capital-abundant, another attribute of industrial leadership. Computable general equilibrium models have been used to explore what would have happened if France and Sweden had experienced the same 29 percent decline in real grain prices that Britain absorbed (O'Rourke 1997a). The experiment yields an important new insight: cheap grain *increased* real wages in free trade Britain, in the absence of tariffs it would have *reduced* real wages in France, and in the absence of tariffs it would have lowered real wages only modestly in Sweden. Different impacts from the same price shock can be easily reconciled with the sector-specific factors model: cheap grain lowered workers' cost of living economy wide, but reduced the demand for agricultural labor. Where agriculture was a big employer, nominal wages fell economy wide. Where agriculture was a small employer, nominal wages did not fall economy wide. Only 23 percent of the British labor force worked in agriculture in 1871, while the corresponding figure for France was 51 percent. Thus, a negative shock to agricultural labor demand had a much bigger impact on French nominal wages, while the impact on workers' cost of living was about the same.

The economics helps explain why Britain maintained free trade while the continent protected agriculture. Agriculture was a lot less important to the British than to the continental economies. Not only did this imply that cheap grain was better for British than for continental workers, but it also meant that the assets of the rich declined by less (land was a smaller share of total assets), and that agricultural interests had less political clout. Britain and Denmark can be viewed as special cases where their economic structure ensured that grain invasion had a less profound political impact than in other European countries. It appears that much of the variation in European trade policy a century ago can be explained quite adequately by appealing to such factors as the impact of globalization on grain prices and land values, and the impact of cheap food on real wages.

3.7 Using history to inform policy

The standard view of history seems to be that there was an exogenous collapse of the global economy after 1914, a de-globalization implosion driven by two world wars, two periods of fragile peace, a great depression, and a cold war (e.g, Sachs and Warner 1995a). The late twentieth century has marked a successful struggle to reconstruct that pre-World War I global economy. Basically, this view of history treats these spectacular changes in global policy as revolutionary switches in regime that were pretty much independent of economic events and thus to be taken as exogenous.

This view ignores the fact that immigration policy in labor-scarce parts of the global economy became increasingly restrictive prior to 1914, and that much of this retreat from open immigration policies was driven by a defense of the deteriorating relative economic position of the working poor in the labor-scarce New World. It also ignores the fact that liberal attitudes toward trade were brief, and that protection rose sharply almost everywhere on the European continent from the 1870s onwards. Much of this retreat from free trade was manifested by protection of domestic agriculture from the negative price shocks associated with globalization. And most of this retreat from free trade was driven by a defense of the trade-induced deterioration in the relative economic position of both the landed rich at the top and the landless poor at the bottom.

A late nineteenth-century globalization backlash made a powerful contribution to interwar de-globalization. Is this history likely to repeat? Maybe not. After all, the migrations from poor to rich countries today are pretty trivial compared with the mass migrations of a century ago, and governments today have far more sophisticated ways to compensate losers than they had a century ago. Yet, history does supply a warning: there is an endogenous globalization backlash in our past that could reappear in our future.

References

Abramovitz, M. 1986. "Catching Up, Forging Ahead, and Falling Behind." *Journal of Economic History*, 46 June: 385–406.

Aghion, P. 1997. "Inequality and Economic Growth." in this volume.

Ahluwalia, M. S. 1976. "Inequality, Poverty and Development." *Journal of Development Economics*, 3, 4: 307–342.

Alesina, A. and Perotti, R. 1994. "The Political Economy of Growth: A Critical Survey of the Recent Literature." *World Bank Economic Review*, 8, (3): 351–371.

Anderson, J. E. and Neary, J. P. 1994. "Measuring the Restrictiveness of Trade Policy." *The World Bank Economic Review*, 8 (May): 151–169.

Bairoch, P. 1976. "Europe's Gross National Product: 1800–1975." *Journal of European Economic History*, 5 (May–August): 273–340.

Barro, R. J. 1991. "Economic Growth in a Cross Section of Countries." *Journal of Political Economy*, 106 (May): 407–443.

    1996. "The Determinants of Economic Growth." Lionel Robbins Lecture, London School of Economics (February 20–22).

Barro, R. J. and Sala-i-Martin, X. 1992. "Convergence." *Journal of Political Economy*, 100 (April): 223–252.

    1995. *Economic Growth*. McGraw-Hill: New York.

Baumol, W. 1986. "Productivity Growth, Convergence and Welfare: What the Long-Run Data Show," *American Economic Review* 76 (December): 1072–1085.

Baumol, W. J., Blackman, S. A. B., and Wolff, E. N. 1989. *Productivity and American Leadership: The Long View*. MIT Press. Cambridge, Mass.

Bloom, D. E. and Williamson J. G. 1996. "Demographic Transitions, Human Resource Development, and Economic Miracles in Emerging Asia." In J. Sachs and D. Bloom (eds.), *Emerging Asia*. Asian Development Bank, Manila.

    1997. "Demographic Transitions and Economic Miracles in Emerging Asia." NBER Working Paper 6268. National Bureau of Economic Research, Cambridge, Mass.(October).

Borjas, G. 1994. "The Economics of Immigration." *Journal of Economic Literature* 32 (December): 1667–1717.

Borjas, G., Freeman, R. B., and Katz, L. F. 1992. "On the Labor Market Impacts of Immigration and Trade." In G. Borjas and R. B. Freeman (eds.), *Immigration and the Work Force: Economic Consequences for the United States and Source Areas*. University of Chicago Press, Chicago.

Bourguignon, F. and Morrisson, C. 1991. *External Trade and Income Distribution*. OECD, Paris.

Boyer, G. R., Hatton, T. J., and O'Rourke, K. H. 1994. "Emigration and Economic Growth in Ireland, 1850–1914." In T. J. Hatton and J. G. Williamson (eds.), *Migration and the International Labor Market, 1850–1939.* Routledge, London.

Burns, A. 1954. *The Frontiers of Economic Knowledge.* Princeton University Press, Princeton, NJ.

Chandler, A. D. 1977. *The Visible Hand: The Managerial Revolution in American Business.* Belknap Press, Cambridge, Mass.

Collins, W. J. 1997. "When the Tide Turned: Immigration and the Delay of the Great Black Migration." *Journal of Economic History*, 57 (September): 607–632.

Crafts, N. F. R. and Toniolo, G. 1996. *Economic Growth in Europe Since 1945.* Cambridge University Press.

Davis, D. R. 1996. "Trade Liberalization and Income Distribution." Mimeo, Harvard University (June).

Deiniger, K. and Squire, L. 1996. "A New Data Set Measuring Income Inequality." *World Bank Economic Review*, 10 (September): 565–591.

DeLong, J. B. 1988. "Productivity Growth, Convergence and Welfare: Comment." *American Economic Review*, 78 (December): 1138–1154.

Durlauf, S. N. and Johnson, P. 1992. "Local versus Global Convergence Across National Economies." Conference on Economic Fluctuations, National Bureau of Economic Research (July).

Edelstein, M. 1982. *Overseas Investment in the Age of High Imperialism.* Columbia University Press, New York.

Feenstra, R. and Hanson, G. 1995. "Foreign Investment, Outsourcing and Relative Wages." In *Political Economy of Trade Policy: Essays in Honor of Jagdish Bhagwati.* MIT Press, Cambridge, Mass.

Feliciano, Z. 1995. "Workers and Trade Liberalization: The Impact of Trade Reforms in Mexico on Wages and Employment." Mimeo, Queens College.

Flam, H., and Flanders, M. J. 1991. *Heckscher-Ohlin Trade Theory.* MIT Press, Cambridge, Mass.

Freeman, R. 1995. "Are Your Wages Set in Beijing?" *Journal of Economic Perspectives*, 9 (Summer): 15–32.

Girard, L. 1966. "Transport." In H. J. Habbakuk and M. M. Postan (eds.). *The Cambridge Economic History of Europe, Volume VI, The Industrial Revolution and After: Incomes, Population and Technological Change.* Cambridge University Press.

Goldin, C. 1994. "The Political Economy of Immigration Restriction in the United States, 1890 to 1921." In C. Goldin and G. D. Libecap (eds.), *The Regulated Economy: A Historical Approach to Political Economy.* University of Chicago Press, Chicago.

Harley, C. K. 1988. "Ocean Freight Rates and Productivity, 1740–1913: The Primacy of Mechanical Invention Reaffirmed." *Journal of Economic History*, 48: 851–876.

Hatton, T. J. and Williamson, J. G. 1993. "After the Famine: Emigration from Ireland 1850–1913." *Journal of Economic History*, 53: 575–600.

——— 1997. *The Age of Mass Migration: An Economic Analysis.* Oxford University Press, New York.

Kindleberger, C. P. 1951. "Group Behavior and International Trade." *Journal of Political Economy*, 59: 30–46.

Kosters, M. H. 1994. "An Overview of Changing Wage Patterns in the Labor Market." In J. Bhagwati and M. H. Kosters (eds.), *Trade and Wages: Leveling Wages Down?* AEI Press, Washington DC.

Krueger, A. 1978. *Liberalization Attempts and Consequences.* Ballinger, Cambridge.

Krugman, P. and Venables, A. 1995. "Globalization and the Inequality of Nations," NBER Working Paper No. 5098, National Bureau of Economic Research, Cambridge, Mass.

Kuznets, S. 1955. "Economic Growth and Income Inequality." *American Economic Review* 45: 1–28.

Lawrence, L. and Slaughter, M. 1993. "International Trade and American Wages in the 1980s: Giant Sucking Sound or Small Hiccup?" *Brookings Papers on Economic Activity, Microeconomics*, 2: 161–226.

Lindert, P. H. 1994. "Unequal Living Standards." In R. C. Floud and D. N. McCloskey (eds.), *The Economic History of Britain since 1700, Volume I.* Cambridge University Press.

Lindert, P. H. and Williamson, J. G. 1983. "English Workers' Living Standards During the Industrial Revolution: A New Look." *Economic History Review Second Series*, 36 (February): 1–25.

Lucas, R. E. 1988. "On the Mechanics of Economic Development." *Journal of Monetary Economics*, 22 (July): 3–42.

——— 1990. "Why Doesn't Capital Flow from Rich to Poor Countries?" *American Economic Review*, 80 (May): 92–96.

Maddison, A. 1982. *Phases of Capitalist Development.* Oxford University Press.

——— 1989. *The World Economy in the 20th Century.* OECD, Paris.

——— 1991. *Dynamic Forces in Capitalist Development: A Long-Run Comparative View.* Oxford University Press.

——— 1994. "Explaining the Economic Performance of Nations." In W. Baumol, R. Nelson, and E. Wolff (eds.), *Convergence of Productivity: Cross-National Studies and Historical Evidence.* Oxford University Press, New York.

1995. *Monitoring the World Economy 1820–1992.* OECD Development Centre Studies, Paris.

Mankiw, N. G., Romer, D. and Weil, D. N. 1992. "A Contribution to the Empirics of Economic Growth." *Quarterly Journal of Economics,* 107 (May): 407–437.

Mokyr, J. 1990. *The Lever of Riches: Technological Creativity and Economic Progress.* Oxford University Press, New York.

1991. "Dear Labor, Cheap Labor, and the Industrial Revolution." In P. Higonnet, D. S. Landes and H. Rosovsky (eds.), *Favorites of Fortune: Technology, Growth, and Economic Development since the Industrial Revolution.* Harvard University Press, Cambridge, Mass.

Mokyr, J. and ÓGráda, C. 1982. "Emigration and Poverty in Prefamine Ireland." *Explorations in Economic History,* 19(4): 360–384.

Neal, L., and Uselding, P. 1972. "Immigration: A Neglected Source of American Economic Growth: 1790–1912." *Oxford Economic Papers,* 24: 68–88.

Nicholas, S. and Shergold, P. R. 1987. "Human Capital and the Pre-Famine Irish Emigration to England." *Explorations in Economic History,* 24(2): 158–177.

North, D. C. 1958. "Ocean Freight Rates and Economic Development 1750–1913." *Journal of Economic History,* 18: 538–555.

ÓGráda, C. 1994. *Ireland 1780–1939: A New Economic History.* Oxford University Press.

O'Rourke, K. 1992. "Why Ireland Emigrated: A Positive Theory of Factor Flows." *Oxford Economic Papers,* 44: 322–340.

1997a. "The European Grain Invasion, 1870–1913," CER Working Paper WP97/2, Department of Economics, University College Dublin (January).

1997b. "Tariffs and Growth in the Late 19th Century." CER Working Paper WP97/18, Department of Economics, University College Dublin (July).

O'Rourke, K. H., Taylor, A. M., and Williamson, J. G. 1996. "Factor Price Convergence in the Late Nineteenth Century." *International Economic Review,* 37 (August): 499–530.

O'Rourke, K. H. and Williamson, J. G. 1994. "Late 19th Century Anglo-American Factor Price Convergence: Were Heckscher and Ohlin Right?" *Journal of Economic History,* 54 (December): 892–916.

1995. "Open Economy Forces and Late 19th Century Swedish Catch-Up: A Quantitative Accounting." *Scandinavian Economic History Review,* (2): 171–203.

1996. "Education, Globalization, and Catch-Up: Scandinavia in the Swedish Mirror." *Scandinavian Economic History Review*, (3): 287–309.

1997a. *Globalization and History: The Evolution of a 19th Century Atlantic Economy*. MIT Press, Cambridge, Mass.

1997b. "Around the European Periphery 1870–1913: Globalization, Schooling and Growth." *European Review of Economic History*, 1 (August): 153–190.

O'Rourke, K. H., Williamson, J. G., and Hatton, T. J. 1994. "Mass Migration, Commodity Market Integration and Real Wage Convergence." In T. J. Hatton and J. G. Williamson (eds.), *Migration and the International Labor Market*, 1850–1939. Routledge, London.

Perotti, R. 1996. "Growth, Income Distribution and Democracy." *Journal of Economic Growth*, 1 (June): 149–187.

Pollard, S. 1978. "Labour in Great Britain." In P. Mathias and M. M. Postan (eds.), *The Cambridge Economic History of Europe: Volume VII: The Industrial Economies: Capital, Labour, and Enterprise, Part I.* Cambridge University Press.

Richardson, J. D. 1995. "Income Inequality and Trade: How to Think, What to Conclude." *Journal of Economic Perspectives*, 9 (Summer): 33–55.

Robbins, D. 1996. "Trade, Trade Liberalization and Inequality in Latin America and East Asia – Synthesis of Seven Countries." Harvard Institute for International Development, mimeo (March).

Rogowski, R. 1989. *Commerce and Coalitions: How Trade Affects Domestic Political Arrangements*. Princeton University Press, Princeton, NJ.

Romer, P. 1986. "Increasing Returns and Long-Run Growth." *Journal of Political Economy*, 94 (October): 1002–1037.

1989. "Capital Accumulation in the Theory of Long-Run Growth." In R. J. Barro (ed.), *Modern Business Cycle Theory*. Harvard University Press, Cambridge, Mass.

Sachs, J. D. and Warner, A. 1995a. "Economic Reform and the Process of Global Integration." *Brookings Papers on Economic Activity, I.* Brookings Institution, Washington DC.

1995b. "Natural Resource Abundance and Economic Growth." NBER Working Paper No. 5398, National Bureau of Economic Research, Cambridge, Mass. (December).

Solow, R. M. 1956. "A Contribution to the Theory of Economic Growth." *Quarterly Journal of Economics*, 70 (February): 65–94.

Summers, R. and Heston, A. 1991. "The Penn World Table (Mark 5): An Expanded Set of International Comparisons, 1950–1988." *Quarterly Journal of Economics*, 106 (May): 327–368.

Taylor, A. M. 1996. "International Capital Mobility in History: The Saving-Investment Relationship." NBER Working Paper 5743, National Bureau of Economic Research, Cambridge, Mass. (September).

Taylor, A. M., and Williamson, J. G. 1997. "Convergence in the Age of Mass Migration." *European Review of Economic History*, 1 (April): 27–63.

Timmer, A. and Williamson, J. G. 1996. "Racism, Xenophobia or Markets? The Political Economy of Immigration Policy Prior to the Thirties." NBER Working Paper No. 5867, National Bureau of Economic Research, Cambridge, Mass. (December).

1997. "Immigration Policy Prior to the Thirties: Labor Markets, Policy Interactions and Globalization Backlash." Department of Economics, Harvard University (March).

Williamson, J. G. 1974. *Late Nineteenth Century American Development: A General Equilibrium History.* Cambridge University Press.

1982. "Immigrant-Inequality Trade Offs in the Promised Land: Income Distribution and Absorptive Capacity Prior to the Quotas." In B. Chiswick (ed.), *The Gateway: U.S. Immigration Issues and Policies.* American Enterprise Institute, Washington DC.

1986. "The Impact of the Irish on British Labor Markets During the Industrial Revolution." *Journal of Economic History*, 46: 693–720.

1993. "Human Capital Deepening, Inequality, and Demographic Events Along the Asia Pacific Rim." In G. Jones, N. Ogawa, and J. G. Williamson (eds.). *Human Resources and Development Along the Asia-Pacific Rim.* Oxford University Press.

1995. "The Evolution of Global Labor Markets Since 1830: Background Evidence and Hypotheses." *Explorations in Economic History*, 32: 141–196.

1996. "Globalization, Convergence and History." *Journal of Economic History*, 56 (June): 1–30.

1997a. "Globalization and Inequality, Past and Present." *World Bank Research Observer*, 12 (August): 117–135.

1997b. "Growth, Inequality, Demography and History," invited address to the Third World Cliometrics Conference, Munich (July).

Williamson, J. G. and Lindert, P. H. 1980. *American Inequality: A Macroeconomic History.* Academic Press, New York.

Wolff, E. N. 1991. "Capital Formation and Productivity Convergence Over the Long Term." *American Economic Review*, 81 (June): 565–579.

Wood, A. 1994. *North-South Trade, Employment and Inequality: Changing Fortunes in a Skill-Driven World.* Clarendon Press, Oxford.

Wright, G. 1986. *Old South, New South: Revolutions in the Southern Economy Since the Civil War.* Oxford University Press, New York.

1990. "The Origins of American Industrial Success, 1879–1940." *American Economic Review*, 80 (September): 651–668.

Zevin, R. B. 1992. "Are World Financial Markets More Open? If So, Why and With What Effects?" In T. Banuri and J. B. Schor (eds.), *Financial Openness and National Autonomy: Opportunities and Constraints.* Clarendon Press, Oxford.

Author index

Subject index

Abramovitz, Moses, 108, 109, 110, 125–6, 129, 130n
age-related wage differentials, 35, 38
Aghion, Philippe, 14, 16, 18, 21, 24, 25, 48n, 58n, 72n, 75n, 77n, 98, 112
AK growth model, 14–17, 18, 19, 28, 29, 87

Bacchetta, P., 27
Bairoch, Paul, 120, 127
Banerjee, A., 24, 25, 27
Baumol, William, 18, 108, 109, 110, 125–6, 128, 129
Borjas, George, 42n, 155, 156, 172, 173–4
Boyer, George, 146, 147, 148, 149
Bretton Woods, 130

canal transport, 133–4, 190
capital accumulation, 133, 143, 167
capital flows, 112, 113, 132, 167–8
    government intervention in, 130
    mobility of, 149–50, 151, 153, 168, 174
capital market imperfections, 13, 15–19, 24, 31, 32
    incentives as source of, 18, 19, 21
Chandler, Alfred, 134
Cobden-Chevalier Treaty 1860, 176
commodities, 105, 130, 131

price equalization of, 126, 136–7, 138, 139, 168, 176, 190
    within Atlantic economy, 136–7, 141
    within national markets, 136, 141, 142, 190
Common Agricultural Policy (European), 190
computer expenditure, 47
conditional growth models, 107–8, 127
convergence
interwar cessation of, 128–31, 182–3
    as recent phenomenon, 109–10, 115
Corn Laws (UK), 113
corporate governance, 11
credit
    availability of, 16, 18, 82
    cycles, 24, 26
credit-market imperfections, 11, 18, 22, 25, 28, 31

diminishing returns to capital, 13–14, 14–15, 17, 18, 31, 32, 33

education levels, as measure of inequality, 9, 34–8, 42n, 44, 47, 48, 54, 55, 58, 60–4, 76, 80, 72
    see also labor supply

203